A Developmental Approach to Early Numeracy

Tops

A Developmental Approach to Early Numeracy

Helping to raise children's achievements and deal with difficulties in learning

Carol Aubrey

QUESTIONS
PUBLISHING
COMPANY

First published in 1999
by The Questions Publishing Company Ltd
27 Frederick Street, Birmingham B1 3HH

Designed by Al Stewart
Cover design by James Davies
Illustrations by Martin Cater

ISBN 1-84190-009-5

Acknowledgement

Extracts from *Wis en Reken*, materials, by H. Boswinkel *et al.* appear courtesy of the publishers, Uitgeverij Bekadidact, Utrecht.

Contents

Introduction

The challenge of teaching diverse pupil groups

INTERNATIONAL comparison in mathematics education continues to provoke debate and has had a real impact on practice. This is reflected most recently in policy-makers' preoccupation with a back-to-basics curriculum and a greater emphasis on mental calculation and whole-class teaching with the introduction of the new national numeracy strategy in September 1999. This is intended to reduce the wide variation in attainment between English pupils of the same age whether resulting from developmental differences or delay and whether cognitive or social in origin.

The structured daily lessons of 45–60 minutes are central to the government's target to bring 75 per cent of eleven-year-olds up to the expected standard in mathematics, that is level four, by the year 2002. Recently published primary league tables show that only 59 per cent of children had reached the target in 1998, so schools will be under pressure to implement the new mathematics framework (DfEE, 1999) in order to meet their own numeracy targets which are to be agreed with local authorities.

There is evidence already to show that schools taking part in the numeracy pilot strategy made significant progress in both English and mathematics (a 9 per cent improvement in the proportion of children achieving the expected norm for eleven-year-olds). This is in spite of the fact that the schools taking part were not representative: they were in disadvantaged areas and had twice the national average intake of pupils receiving free meals. Whilst the project is judged to have improved mental arithmetic teaching and provided an appropriate structure, there was still a wide gap between the highest and lowest achieving schools, which an OFSTED report (1999) has warned is likely to be replicated across the country when all schools are involved in the strategy.

The numeracy task force, however, has taken a strong lead by:

- including special schools in the framework;
- encouraging schools to include the Special Educational Needs Co-ordinator (SENCO) in the initial, three-day training conference;
- ensuring the programme for reception classes takes account of the new early learning goals for three- to five-year-olds and provides a bridge from the goals to the National Curriculum;
- recommending that the Basic Skills Agency extend and develop its Family Numeracy programme and ensure that the activities are linked closely to children's progress in school.

Moreover, the Department for Education and Employment (DfEE) has sponsored local education authority (LEA) bids for pilot projects to support the development of numeracy skills at key stage 3 (for twelve- to fourteen-year-olds). Among factors identified as promoting high standards of numeracy in the framework are:

- assessment to identify strengths and weaknesses to set group and individual targets;
- controlled differentiation, with suitable objectives incorporated into individual education programmes (IEPs).

The findings of the pilot strategy – that groups who made most progress had initially the lowest scores – are encouraging. Dutch mathematics educators have noted, however, that reform takes time, and in fact they still regard their curriculum reform of some thirty years as 'work under construction'. In particular they have recently acknowledged the need to differentiate still more clearly minority groups, including special needs children. The growth of children's knowledge and understanding of mathematics as a human activity, they claim, can never be 'fixed or finished' (van den Heuvel-Panhuizen, 1998).

With that humbling thought in mind this book will attempt to confront some of the issues associated with teaching numeracy to diverse pupil groups in a context of curriculum change. It proposes the view that if children enter school with varying levels of development, which some would argue school-based attempts are unable to overcome or blur, then an essential strategy in accommodating to these differences will be to take children's existing knowledge and strategies as a starting point for instruction. The OFSTED report (1999) tends to focus on the quality of teaching and school management in order to account for low achievement in mathematics. This book will argue that teaching and learning are inextricably linked and that connecting what is taught to what is known already is the best way to stimulate further development. Accordingly, the first chapter will examine the current context to teaching and learning and, in particular, consider the role of the SENCO in this. Chapters 2–5 will then examine how children's informal and school-related strategies develop, and how the class teacher can take account of these. The implications of this for the numeracy strategy are that very clearly targeted work will need to be prepared for individuals, pairs or small groups in order for progress to be made. In terms of the SENCO's role in curriculum planning and assessment in the school as a whole, better numeracy standards occur when:

> Assessments are used to identify pupils' strengths and difficulties, to set group and individual targets for them to achieve and to plan the next stage of work . . . assessments include informal observations and oral questioning, regular mental tests, and half-termly planned activities to judge progress.
>
> Where teaching is concerned question pupils effectively . . . giving

them time to think before answering, targeting individuals to take account of their attainment and needs, asking them to demonstrate and explain their methods and reasoning, and exploring reasons for any wrong answers . . . including some non-routine problems that require them to think for themselves . . . ensure that differentiation is manageable . . . with targeted, positive support to help those who have difficulties with mathematics to keep up with their peers. (DfEE, 1999: 5)

Each of the five chapters in the book provides examples of lessons, based on the following learning strands:

- counting;
- memorising of addition and subtraction facts to 10 and 20;
- multiplication and division tables;
- mental arithmetic;
- column arithmetic;
- fractions, decimals, percentages and ratio.

The activities are in the main inspired by the Dutch approach to primary maths – 'realistic mathematics' – which has been shown to raise achievement across all levels of ability in primary maths classes.

References
Department for Education and Employment (DfEE) (1999) *The National Numeracy Strategy*, London: DfEE.
van den Heuvel-Panhuizen, M. (1998) 'Realistic mathematics education: work in progress', paper presented at the Nordic Mathematics Association Conference (NORMA, 5–9 June, Kristiansand, Norway.

Chapter 1

Mathematics and the role of the SENCO

Introduction

ACCORDING to the Education Act 1993 and the Code of Practice (DfEE, 1993), a key purpose of the SENCO is to ensure that the school's special educational needs (SEN) policy and practices identify and meet the needs of all pupils and result in improved standards of achievement. More recently new standards have been set for initial teacher training and continuing professional development: *Teaching: High Status, High Standards, Requirements for Courses for Initial Teacher Training* (DfEE, 1998a); and *National Professional Standards for Teachers and Headteachers* (TTA, 1998). The first of these sets standards for the award of qualified teacher status, initial teacher training in mathematics and in information and communication technology. Whilst it is beyond the scope of this chapter to give a full account of the standards for mathematics teaching, it is certainly important to consider the issues raised with respect to special needs. The TTA document requires the headteacher to know about the implications of teaching pupils with special needs throughout the school to:

> A. ensure that improvements in literacy, numeracy and informational technology are priority targets for all pupils, including those with special educational needs;
> B. monitor and evaluate the quality of teaching and standards of learning and achievement of all pupils, including those with special educational or linguistic needs, in order to set and meet challenging, realistic targets for improvement. (TTA, 1998: s. 5)

Furthermore, under standards for subject leaders, there is an expectation that they too will understand the needs of all learners, including those with SEN, on coverage, continuity, progression, expectations and targets. Subject leaders, moreover, are asked 'to work with the SENCO and any other staff with special education needs expertise, to ensure that individual education plans are used to set subject-specific targets and match work well to pupils' needs'. At the same time the expectation is still that the SENCO is the one who really understands about the teaching and learning of SEN children in the school. In practice, however, unless the SENCO and, in this case, the mathematics co-ordinator do work together in the early stages of the Code of Practice, the teaching of numeracy, never mind mathematics, will lack coherence in provision and uncertainty in responsibility for the development of practice across the range of attainments, including special needs. In this respect it is interesting to note that national standards for initial teacher training in mathematics make *no* reference to SEN. On the other hand, realistic standards in SEN in relation to information and communication technology (ICT) are set for initial teacher training. Standards for the award of qualfied teacher status also require knowledge of the Code of Practice for SEN, identification of pupils who have SEN and how to get help in order to 'give positive and targeted support'. More recently the TTA has proposed standards for specialist SEN teachers, and training which is aimed at those who regularly teach pupils with severe and complex needs. Moderate learning difficulties are not included, however, since it is assumed that pupils with general learning difficulties are increasingly being supported in ordinary schools. So how, then, does the SENCO discharge the responsibility for the day-to-day operation of school mathematics provision for pupils with SEN?

The White Paper *Excellence in Schools* (DfEE, 1997b) set out the Labour government's policy aim of raising standards in education not just for the few top pupils but for the many who are currently low-achieving. In other words, there are at present believed to be unacceptable differences in attainment among different groups of children in schools. As the Green Paper *Excellence for All Children* (DfEE, 1997a) indicated, special needs children are an integral part of this strategy to raise standards in both mainstream and special schools.

One aspect of this strategy must be the exploration of new approaches to organising classrooms to meet the needs of a wide range of pupils, as well as more effective methods of teaching and learning which focus, in particular, on literacy, numeracy and information technology. In fact providing effective baseline assessment for all children entering primary schools has already been introduced so that their progress can be more effectively judged, and at least one hour each day is being devoted to both literacy and numeracy in every primary school. The provision of early, high-quality intervention is intended to reduce the number of children who need long-term special education provision; and to divert attention away from procedural aspects and the paperwork associated with the Code of Practice which can 'fill time and dominate attention'.

National guidelines and training for all primary teachers in best practice in the teaching of literacy and numeracy are intended to improve children's achievements by the end of primary schooling to meet national targets. In fact, target-setting in both mainstream and special schools will take explicit account of the scope for improving achievements, and there will be higher expectations of the standards that children can achieve. The discussion of expectations and target-setting, however, leads us back to the consideration of the essential teaching skills and strategies required to meet children's diverse needs. The consultation paper on *National Guidelines for the Special Educational Needs Co-ordinator* stated that:

> SENCOs should have knowledge and understanding of the teaching of pupils with SEN and the main strategies for improving and sustaining high standards of teaching, learning and pupil achievement. (TTA, 1997: 12)

Systems for identifying, assessing and providing high-quality teaching based on sound subject knowledge, with appropriate monitoring and reviewing of progress, as well as effective dissemination of this expertise, are central to these new SEN policies.

As even a cursory glance over special needs publications in general will reveal, the majority of research and writing in the area of learning difficulties concerns literacy rather than numeracy, in spite of growing public concern about falling standards in literacy *and* numeracy over the 1990s, stimulated by the so-called 'Three Wise Men Report' of Alexander *et al.* (1992). More comprehensive data have become available as National Curriculum standard assessment tasks (SATs) have been introduced for seven- and eleven-year-olds and the results of two international studies of mathematics and science have been published.

These data have demonstrated that there are solid grounds for the concern expressed about standards in mathematics. The Third International Mathematics and Science Study (TIMSS) published during the summer of 1997 (Harris *et al.*, 1997) showed that the performance of English nine-year-olds was significantly below the international mean in mathematics. Similarly, at the national level, the results of SATs in mathematics for eleven-year-olds showed that only 62 per cent of pupils reached the target of level four or above in 1997, but that this had dropped to 59 per cent in 1998. The annual reports of HM Chief Inspector of Schools, Chris Woodhead, have expressed a continuing concern about standards of achievement and repeatedly called for a 'back to basics' approach. Clearly there is serious underachievement in mathematics, but as yet we have a far from perfect understanding of the conditions that give rise to this, or to the more serious and long-term disabilities in mathematics suffered by a special subset of children.

Over the last twenty or so years, however, there has been a growing research base devoted to the study of children's early development of number, arithmetic and mathematical problem-solving and the ways that this is expressed in different cultures. This first chapter will show how a developmental approach can help to identify children with learning disabilities in mathematics and provide a more accurate conceptualisation of their difficulties.

The goal of this chapter, which focuses on the SENCO's role, is to consider ways to identify, to understand and to help children with low achievement or specific learning difficulty in mathematics. In fact, by taking a developmental perspective and drawing on research concerning normally developing children, there is much that the SENCO can discover about learning difficulty in mathematics. With this enhanced professional knowledge the SENCO can then reflect upon the characteristics of effective teaching and learning for SEN pupils, and think constructively about the nature and origins of, as well as appropriate interventions for, learning difficulties in mathematics.

Accordingly the chapter will:

- examine the informal mathematical knowledge young children develop in out-of-school contexts;
- consider the misunderstandings that can occur when this knowledge comes up against formal school mathematics;
- outline some of the strategies which can be devised to identify those needing special teaching; and
- evaluate the success of those strategies in fostering pupils' progress, self-esteem and confidence.

Pre-school maths

Whatever the social, cultural or racial group to which children belong they will grow up in a social and physical world which is rich in quantitative information and mathematical experiences. They see numerals on clocks, calendars, buses, houses, telephones, televisions and in books. They will manipulate, rearrange and count small, discrete objects of varying amounts. They observe that containers in the kitchen hold volumes of differing amounts and see that money in shops is counted and exchanged. Whilst the quantitative environments of young children vary, they all have opportunities to count and compare objects, to increase and decrease the sizes of small sets of objects and to hear nursery rhymes such as 'Sing a song of sixpence' and fairy tales such as *Goldilocks and the Three Bears* which describe quantitative events and experiences. Human language, in fact, carries the means to describe the quantitative experiences that children encounter.

Research suggests that even infants and very small children have an early, intuitive grasp that addition increases small quantities and subtraction decreases them. As Geary (1994) has outlined, children universally use their culture's counting systems to carry out arithmetical calculations and, in the early stages, rely on body parts, such as fingers, to support their counting. This early knowledge is personal and idiosyncratic since it is not encoded in a formal mathematical language or notation system. It has been described by Vygotskii (1978) as 'spontaneous' rather than 'scientific'. For instance, children recognise some numerals which have a personal significance for them and invent their own systems for other numerals which they do not know; for example, writing: '123' for three; and '1234 |||' for seven.

Figure 1.1

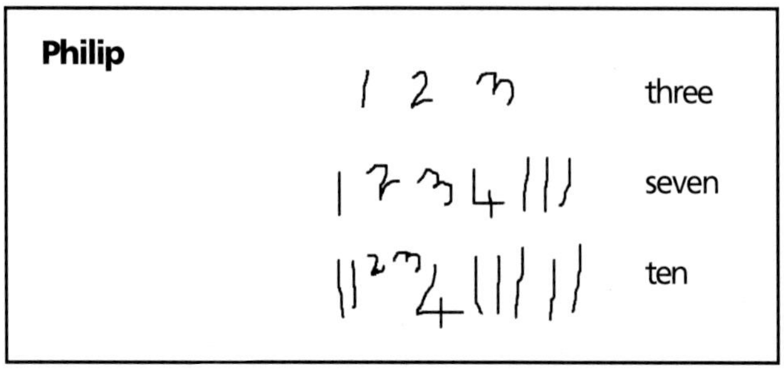

When formal knowledge runs out they might invent a system to represent the quantity in question with tally marks. For three-dimensional shapes, to take another example, young children will mix formal language with their everyday understanding, so a cube may be described as a 'square block', a cuboid as a 'rectangle like a long brick' or a pyramid as 'pointy and like a triangle . . . like those things where camels are . . . pyramids!' These examples serve to illustrate how children actively construct their mathematical thinking and understanding, and the personal yet powerful knowledge base which is available to them and which serves as the basis for later school learning.

Figure 1.2

Using words to describe common 3-dimensional shapes, show the child (in turn) the cube, the cuboid, the cylinder, the cone, the triangular prism, and the triangular pyramid.

Say: 'What can you tell me about this? What does it look like? Offer one further prompt: anything else?'

1   Cube: . . . .
2   Cuboid: . . . .
3   Cylinder: . . . .
4   Cone: . . . .
5   Triangular prism: . . . .
6   Triangular pyramid: . . . .

Note what the child says and does in response to being presented with each shape.

As young as two years children will recognise that adding or removing one from a very small set of objects changes the set size. By four to five years they can solve simple calculation problems involving small sets of objects, provided that they can carry out the action embodied in the problem. Children's ideas and responses to 'more' and 'less', adding to or taking away objects from a set, their perception of shape, size and volume are, however, tied to a specific context or set of circumstances, and this has led psychologists to describe this informal mathematical knowledge as 'situated cognition'.

Despite cultural variation in the rate and overall level of achievement, general similarities in arithmetical calculation can be observed as children move through stages of counting objects, counting fingers and verbal counting (first, counting out both numbers separately before counting altogether, then counting on from the first of two numbers in a sum regardless of its size and, finally, counting on from the largest number). Later, children will decompose one or both numbers to make an easier 'sum': for example, $9 + 8 = (9 + 1) + 7$ or $10 + 7$, and eventually retrieving number facts from long-term memory.

This knowledge takes a number of years to develop and it is not a simple linear process. Children construct new strategies, refine or cast aside old ones while the balance or 'mix' of strategies gradually shifts towards more efficient, retrieval-based strategies. These strategies represent not only observable problem-solving methods but also mental operations or 'schema' (conceptual knowledge) as well as memory representations (procedural or routine knowledge) and their interactions. A schema refers to a unit of knowledge which can be internalised. This could be about objects, situations, processes and actions, or an organised structure which summarises knowledge about cases or instances, linked on the basis of their similarity or difference.

As soon as arithmetic problem-solving moves beyond the simple calculations which can be modelled easily with manipulatives it is not as straightforward. For example, Jason has seven sweets, if he eats three he will have as many as Amy. How many does Amy have? Just as the child needs a range of basic number and counting skills to carry out simple arithmetical calculations, for problem-solving a range of additional skills is required. These include comprehension (reading comprehension in the case of written problems); the ability to translate the problem 'text' into an arithmetic operation (in the case of written problems, into an arithmetic or algebraic equation); and 'metacognitive' skills, for thinking about and deciding which strategy to select. Comprehending a problem entails not just good reading skills and a basic mathematical vocabulary but also the recognition that keywords carry a special mathematical meaning, such as 'more' means addition in: 'Ben has two sweets, Charlotte gave him two more, so how many does he have now?' Equally important is an understanding of the relationships described in the problem in order to translate them into an operation or equation. To illustrate the complexity of this, in 'Charlotte has five sweets and Ben has two, so how many more sweets does Charlotte have than Ben?' the child has to *subtract* although the 'more' suggests addition. Problem-solving thus requires the careful mental manipulation of information in order to translate it into a familiar operation. This means that mental representation and working memory resources are also involved, as well as comprehension and basic computational skills.

While the simple counting skills of young children are adequate to solve everyday, concrete problems, more complex problems require not only more sophisticated arithmetic skills but a range of other skills. Moreover, whilst skilled problem-solving rests on a foundation of arithmetic skills, it is essential to recognise the close relationship between the two. This overview gives some indication both of the rich informal knowledge which children bring into school and of the complexity – and, hence, potential for confusion – of the early, and seemingly straightforward, stages of children's arithmetic and problem-solving which are often taken for granted.

Lessons from abroad

In most cultures children enter school with a practical informal understanding of mathematics which they learn while making sense of their social world. One task for the teacher, then, is to build on this prior knowledge in order to induct children into the formal system of written and academic mathematics. In fact, since children continue to develop informal knowledge, the teacher continues to need to have access to the methods and strategies they are using since these provide a window on their current understanding and the basis for further teaching.

Making effective links to this informal knowledge constitutes the fundamental challenge to teaching. It is one to which we shall return later. First, though, what exactly is the nature of mathematics teaching in this country? In May 1997, soon after the general election, the new Labour government announced targets for children's achievements in mathematics (specifically, the number of eleven-year-old children reaching Level 4 or above was to be raised from 55 to 75 per cent by 2002). The chair of a new task force for numeracy, Professor David Reynolds, made it clear that it was important for England and Wales to look to 'lessons from abroad' for guidance on lesson content and teaching method. The TIMSS data referred to earlier emphasised the important role in high achievement played by whole-class teaching, as well as by individualisation in mathematics teaching and regular homework. In terms of organisation in this country, however, the TIMSS data revealed that the most frequent form of classroom grouping was for pupils to work individually with the assistance of the class teacher, and that whole-class teaching, by contrast, was less frequent in England and Wales than in any other participating country.

Much has been made in the media of whole-class, so-called 'interactive' teaching, where teachers ask open and closed questions, seek children's explanations for the strategies they use and analyse the nature of their errors. Such teaching is most closely associated with the Pacific Rim countries, which have consistently topped the international league tables for mathematics achievement. But, in fact, it is also characteristic of many of our closer European neighbours. In relation to the effective classroom processes of high-achieving European cultures, Bierhoff (1996), for instance, has reported a greater emphasis on mental calculation in continental schools; on core textbooks and teachers' guides which provide detailed and graded teaching steps, with special practice exercises at each; and emphasis on whole-number arithmetic, which is seen as the foundation upon which later mathematics is built. Our own National Curriculum in mathematics is broader in scope, including shape and space and handling data, which was until recently the province of secondary schooling. It has been subject to four major revisions in the last nine years. There is a plethora of published materials, giving teachers wide choice in the selection and preparation of teaching materials. TIMSS noted that as a result children have learned largely by themselves, often choosing their own strategies and with limited teacher contact.

Whilst Asian and continental teaching stresses oral methods of calculation to stimulate the development of 'automatisation' of number facts, our teaching has stressed written calculation. (Note the photographs of three- and four-year-olds carrying out written tasks in Basic Skills Agency's 1998 publication, *Family Numeracy Adds Up*, and the messages which this conveys about our values and our understanding of the nature of learning by four-year-olds in school.) By contrast, high-achieving cultures of Europe and the Far East have generated a 'learning culture' where achievement is institutionalised in schools, and there is a centralised system of education which provides clear guidelines on curriculum textbooks and assessment, delivered to relatively homogeneous groups of children. The national numeracy strategy has to a large extent used the experiences of these countries as an examplar.

Our own recent British Council-sponsored, comparative study of two contrasting European countries (England and Slovenia) – one with international achievement scores for mathematics significantly below and one above the international mean – has revealed similar trends. In summary we found:

- the performance of English six-year-old school pupils, for speed and accuracy of arithmetic calculation and problem-solving, was superior to Slovene pre-schoolers of the same age;
- within a year, through emphasis in teaching on accurate oral arithmetical calculation, seven-year-old Slovene pupils had caught up, and by eight years had forged ahead, and there were significant differences at ages nine and ten;
- English pupils had a slight advantage in problem-solving, reflecting the greater emphasis in our teaching on the application of calculation strategies.

Detailed analysis of individual children's strategies in a mental calculation task showed some evidence that the English six- and seven-year-olds continued to develop accuracy and fluency in their strategies. Thereafter, the attainment gap between English high and low attainers widened. Although there was some evidence of increased accuracy in carrying out tasks in simple mental addition, multiplication and division, the inaccuracy and lack of effective strategies for subtraction in both high and low attainers were very marked at all ages from eight to eleven years. Clinical interviews revealed that most older pupils reached accurate solutions for addition problems by carrying out the formal, written algorithm in their heads rather than by using flexible transformations of numbers and fact retrieval. For example, when presented with a card reading: '25 + 58' and the words 'Can you tell me the answer to this sum?', Andrew (nine years old) said: '83 . . . I said 5 and 8 makes 13 . . . 2 and 5 makes 7 and 1 more . . . is 8, so 83.' Similar results were obtained from both pilot and main phases of the project, suggesting that the observed differences did, indeed, reflect different emphases in mathematics teaching and curriculum of the two nations.

But what can be learned specifically from the English perspective? Competent problem-solving rests upon sound arithmetic skills, as outlined earlier.

Improving problem-solving cannot be achieved *instead* of teaching basic arithmetic but rather *in addition to* basic counting, number and arithmetical skills. In the current educational climate, however, it is important not to lose sight of what we have achieved in the area of mathematical investigations and problem-solving for this may well underly our better showing internationally in standards for science.

In summary, we find that although English children enter school with a developed informal mathematical knowledge, many have difficulty with formal mathematics. These difficulties accumulate over the years, sapping confidence and draining esteem and motivation. In our own study, it was very noticeable that low achievers were reluctant to talk about their strategies and, when observed, some were unwilling to use their fingers to support counting. By the time the results of our project were published and before the TIMSS findings had been made available, the government set up a numeracy task force and a national numeracy project.

A new approach

The National Numeracy Project was set up by the DfEE in September 1996, under the direction of Anita Straker, in partnership with OFSTED, the then Schools Curriculum and Assessment Authority (SCAA), the Teacher Training Agency (TTA) and the Basic Skills Agency. Pilot local authorities each set up a local centre for numeracy and appointed consultants to work with groups of schools. The project scheme:

- involved pupils in 1000 schools on a rolling, two-year programme;
- provided training for the mathematics co-ordinators and senior management;
- ensured free supply cover while teachers underwent this training;
- carried out a whole-school audit and provided free project materials and familiarisation with the project's curriculum framework.

The project provided an outline for the national numeracy hour, which included:

- an initial, ten-minute instruction and whole-class interactive, mental-calculation session, in which precise vocabulary was developed;
- a main teaching activity for groups of four to six children, where differentiation was planned (with both a modified and an extended version of the main task);
- a final plenary session where children shared, explained and demonstrated their work and the class teacher reviewed and/or set new targets; and
- consolidation work either in the form of homework or follow-up class work as an important characteristic.

Where possible the 'warm-up' period was related to the main part of the lesson. Careful planning of the distribution of the teacher-focus group had to take place, as well as the establishment of ground rules for working and the use of materials, which were formally taught. The plenary session needed skilful handling to identify key learning points, to stimulate pupil reflection and to draw together the main threads of the lesson in a 'pacey' manner. The style and content of work was much influenced by continental methods of teaching. When the numeracy task force made its final recommendations in the summer of 1998, these were accepted in full by the government and £60 million of support was pledged to provide training and support for all teachers, building on best practice, particularly from the numeracy project:

> The key objective is to provide good quality teaching in a daily mathematics lesson in all schools with primary-aged pupils by Autumn 1999. The daily lessons will last from 45 to 60 minutes depending on the age of the pupils and will include regular oral and mental work. Teachers will spend more time teaching the whole class together, engaging pupils with clear instruction and using effective questioning. Pupils will also spend time working together in groups and pairs . . . The strategy's training and support will extend to maintained special schools, though some . . . aspects . . . will need to be adapted to meet children's particular needs. (DfEE, 1998b: 2)

Up to 300 local authority numeracy consultants have been recruited to support training from 1 April 1999, together with local 'leading mathematics teachers'. An initial three-day training course for the headteacher, mathematics co-ordinator and one other (presumably the SENCO) has already been held, with a governor representative invited for one day. Training has taken place during three in-service training (INSET) days, with a further five days of release time to allow teachers to watch demonstration lessons and for the mathematics co-ordinator and the SENCO to work with colleagues. For the SENCO this requires close collaboration with senior members of staff as well as the mathematics and assessment co-ordinators. As Merttens (1997) has indicated, interactive teaching is not a return to telling; it requires not only instructing and explaining but dialogue between teacher and pupils. INSET should therefore make use of modelling good lessons, versatile teaching strategies and effective management and control. The daily mental mathematics session, for instance, comprises short, teacher-focused question-and-answer exchanges, using open and closed questions, to develop children's mental, numerical strategies. Numeracy lessons include the application of number in measures, geometry and data handling. Resources consist of simple number lines and grids, a cloth bag and dice, and a flip chart for the warm-up period. Textbooks with good graded practice materials in numeracy can be used to follow up the mental strategies introduced and modelled in the ten-minute sessions. For instance, skip-counting in twos and threes, up and down (2, 4, 6 . . . ; 3, 6, 9 . . .) can be followed up with written sums (3 + 2, 8 + 2, 11 + 2 . . . ; 3 + 3, 8 + 3, 11 + 3) and so on.

The description of mathematics education in this country as it has been, compared with other countries, and as it will be, when reformed in the light of 'lessons from abroad', serves to underline the fact that children's learning of mathematics cannot be understood in isolation from the culture, the schools, the teaching and the curriculum which constitute the broader ecology in which it is embedded. That said, there are still children who, despite cultural and educational opportunities, fail to make expected progress, and it is to these children we turn in the next section.

Identifying and assessing children with learning difficulties

Children with serious learning difficulties in mathematics do not learn, despite adequate social and cultural pre-school experiences, initial motivation to succeed and appropriate instruction. It has been estimated that 6 per cent of children may suffer from severe mathematical disabilities, 70 per cent of whom are boys. Strang and Rourke (1985) have suggested three categories of mathematical disability:

- the first involves difficulty in fact retrieval and memory for arithmetic tables;
- the second involves difficulty with procedures and delays in learning basic number skills; and
- the third is a visuo-spatial difficulty in representing and interpreting arithmetical information.

The challenge, then, for the teacher, is two-fold: to distinguish these difficulties from those which result from poor teaching; and then to provide a suitable conceptualisation of the difficulties experienced by such children. This argument hinges upon making a distinction between those who are developmentally *delayed* (as some socio-cultural groups are likely to be); and those who are developmentally *different* (who fail to respond, despite suitable opportunities to learn).

The problem with this argument, however, is that arithmetical calculation and problem-solving depend upon a range of different mental processes. This complexity makes it unlikely that any single cognitive difficulty causes failure in learning mathematics. It may, therefore, be more profitable to examine children's understanding or grasp of the mathematics topics they are currently attempting to master, in order to uncover the gaps or misconceptions they have. It is here that a developmental approach to children's learning is likely to be most fruitful, as certain fundamental questions immediately spring to mind:

- Does the child bring existing informal knowledge to this teaching situation or this formal, written method? (This question does not necessarily apply simply to young children entering school. In order to help older children to recognise that there may be more than one correct procedure, they too will

Figure 1.3

Task: How many skis and how many sticks do skiers have in the gondola?

Show your working

Write how you did it: Answer: 28

14 Ski sticks
14 Skis

4 8 12 16 20 24 28
I counted in my 4xtables up to 7x4

2 + 4 6 8 10 12 14 16 18 20
22 24 26 28

Figure 1.4

Task: Children divided strawberries among themselves fairly. How many strawberries does everybody have?

Show your working:

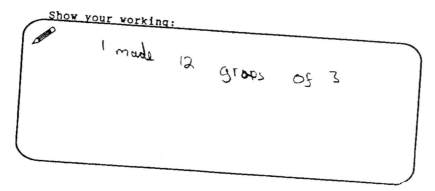

I made 12 groups of 3

Show your working:

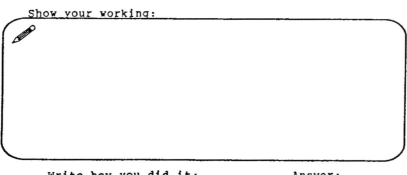

Write how you did it: Answer: 12

I split the strawberry's in to3
and counted how many groups.

Figure 1.5

Task: Children divided strawberries among themselves fairly. How many strawberries does everybody have?

continue to need encouragement both to invent alternative procedures and to share these with others.) See Figures 1.3–1.5.

- Do the child's errors result from systematic errors or 'bugs'? For example, 76 – 29 is not best tackled by decomposing both numbers and over-generalising the rule 'always take the smaller number from the larger one': $(70-20) + (9-6) = 53$.
- Are the strategies unusual or simply immature? For 5 + 5, for instance, one child might count 1, 2, 3, 4, 5, 6, 7, 8, 9, 10; another might simply count on 6,7, 8, 9, 10; whilst a third might retrieve a 'doubles' fact, which is more efficient.
- Is the child having difficulty in remembering basic number facts? (This is, perhaps, the most persistent characteristic of children with learning difficulty in mathematics: Geary, 1993.)

Normally developing children shift gradually from reliance on counting to retrieval of number-fact strategies until retrieval eventually dominates choice. Children with number difficulties rely on more time-consuming counting strategies (Geary *et al.*, 1987) and, when a retrieval strategy is used, they are less likely to be accurate (Geary, 1990). Moreover, as they progress to more efficient count-on strategies they still show a tendency to select ineffective count-all strategies in particular circumstances, suggesting that their grasp of basic counting may still be fragile and unreliable.

- Does the child understand basic mathematical concepts? There is a strong argument here for linking calculation as far as possible to concrete models and situations in teaching and, as noted above, for encouraging children's own invention and discussion of alternative procedures. Conditions related to problem-solving, however, include not only knowledge of mathematical concepts and skill at computation but also general and mathematical reasoning, language skills (vocabulary and reading), memory, attitude towards problem-solving, and even skill at using the structure of a similar, remembered problem – not infrequently cited by primary-aged children as the calculation strategy used.

Specific assessment strategies

National Curriculum assessment is likely already to include portfolio assessment for monitoring progress in relation to curriculum objectives and teaching strategies. It is a useful tool to illuminate the ways children respond, their solution strategies rather than their answers, as well as to evaluate instructional decisions in particular content areas. It is, therefore, important that children's work is collected in a particular time-frame, represents the variety of work situations provided and, if possible, reflects responses to different teaching strategies. For the pupil with learning difficulty in mathematics the items selected must relate to the IEP and include not only the 'raw data' of continuous teacher-assessment described above, but also summarising data, which may include achievement test information as well as anecdotal notes and 'probes' that plot rate and accuracy in particular operations, if precision teaching methods are being used (see Chapter 5).

More important for the investigation of the child's thinking, however, is the clinical interview (Ginsburg *et al.*, 1993). Flexible and non-standardised questions and eliciting 'talk-aloud' methods to examine problem-solving (Schoenfeld, 1985) emerge as the most sensitive and powerful tools to access children's thinking. Consideration of problem-solving, in fact, may be better achieved through detailed observation of groups of children engaged in real-life mathematical problem-solving, possibly with their own self-report (see Figure 1.6). In conjunction with these two methods, interview and observation, 'microgenesis' (Ginsburg, 1997) or repeated observation and interview over time on similar tasks may be employed to complement the portfolio record of children's written responses in order to establish changes over time in the strategy used.

In conclusion, a learning difficulty in mathematics is not absolute and, in fact, may show itself as a difficulty in some areas but not in others. Difficulties may not be general but tied to particular topics, contexts or levels. The developmental perspective outlined here carries the challenge that the difficulty itself may be as much socially constructed inside classrooms as outside. If the difficulty is in one area, there is a case for seeking ways to 'bypass' it. If failure to remember facts is central and persistent, for instance, repeatedly encouraging rote learning is unlikely to be helpful. Mnemonics and flash-card prompts could be used. A number line may help children visualise problems for numbers within 10, within 20 and within 100. For older and more able children a calculator may be used. Learning rules is important; for example, the zero rule (addition involving zero does not change the other number); the number-after rule (one plus the number is the next in the count sequence, such as $3 + 1$ is 4); the skip-next-number rule, which skips the next number ($3 + 1 + 1$ is 5); the commutativity rule, which dictates that order does not affect the sum (so that $5 + 4$ is the same as $4 + 5$); and the ten rule which transforms numbers over 10 to make an easier sum, for instance, $13 + 5 = 10 + (3 + 5) = 18$.

Dutch educators, who have been reforming their mathematics curriculum since the late 1960s, have referred to what they describe as 'didactical assessment' which is intended as a support to the teaching and learning process. This approach is located within a particular view of people and mathematics. According to Freudenthal (1997), mathematics must be connected to reality, stay close to children and be relevant to society in order to be of human value. Mathematics from this point of view involves not subject matter but human activity, with 'mathematisation' as its main characteristic. Teaching mathematics here has a realistic context which confronts children both with problems which are unsolvable as well as with problems with a variety of problem solutions. 'Mathematisation' can occur of different levels which are associated with various levels of understanding through which children pass. These include:

Figure 1.6

Child's self-report

Tick the box which best fits what you thought about your work.

While I was doing these sums/problems I felt:

I was sure that I knew how to do them and I think I could show someone else how to do this sort of sum/problem. ☐

Can you say some more about this?

....

....

....

I know how to do some of the sums/problems, but many I was not sure about. ☐

Can you say some more about this?

....

....

....

I thought that I knew what to do when I started but then I got mixed up and couldn't remember how to do them. ☐

Can you say some more about this?

....

....

....

I was lost from the start. I never understood what the teacher was telling us to do. ☐

Can you say some more about this?

....

....

....

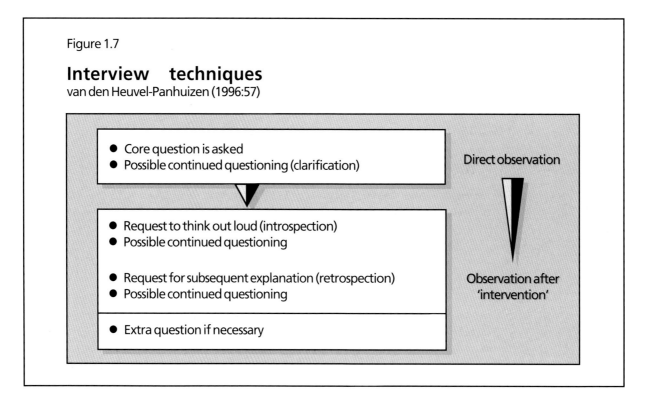

Figure 1.7

Interview techniques
van den Heuvel-Panhuizen (1996:57)

- Core question is asked
- Possible continued questioning (clarification)

Direct observation

- Request to think out loud (introspection)
- Possible continued questioning

- Request for subsequent explanation (retrospection)
- Possible continued questioning

Observation after 'intervention'

- Extra question if necessary

- the ability to invent informal context-related solutions;
- the creation of shortcuts and schematisations;
- the acquisition of insight into underlying principles and, hence, superordinate relationships.

Models can serve as an important bridge between informal context-related mathematics and more formal mathematics. As van den Heuvel-Panhuizen (1996) has indicated, the strength of these models lies not only in their foundation in concrete situations, but also in their inherent flexibility and potential for deployment in high-level mathematics. One of the most powerful models used is the number line, which is described in detail in Chapter 5. This can be introduced in year 2 (for six-year-olds) as a beaded necklace. By year 6 (for eleven-year-olds) it has developed into a double number line for work with fractions and percentages (see examples below, pp. 122–4). Assessment is regarded as important in this context to:

- identify what has been learned; and
- specify how the teaching process can be improved.

For Dutch educators, observations are regarded as providing a holistic picture of the learning process, which involves attending to behaviour, mathematical attitude, solution level, type of errors made, manner of collaboration, need for support, response to prompts, as well as the emotional aspects of motivation and concentration.

This can only occur with open-ended questions in which children work out a problem and construct an answer of their own. These problems are not to be confused with textbook word problems which have as their basis the generation of a conventional operation and accurate response. True reality, they aver, as noted above, has unsolvable or multi-solution problems. For example, van den Heuvel-Panhuizen (1996: 20) illustrates this point with the problem:

> Mr Jensen lives in Utrecht. He must be in Zwolle at 9.00 a.m. on Tuesday morning. Which train should he take? (Check the train timetable.)

This problem cannot be solved out of context, but, at the same time, it does not marginalise children's experience. It requires a solution *attitude* as much as a *method*.

Formal tests are thus regarded as inadequate for diagnosis. They provide 'blindfolded diagnosis' where what counts is incorrect. Realistic alternatives:

- help teachers observe;
- use observation as a departure for text development;
- conduct discussions with the children;
- place more emphasis on formative assessment;
- conduct domain or topic-specific analyses in order to improve teaching goal specification (ibid.: 27).

Observation and interview techniques are fundamental to such practices as they are intended to display children's underlying thought processes and insights. A number of techniques can be used to access these:

- observation;
- introspection (asking the child to think out loud);
- retrospection (asking the child after the event to describe what was done or thought);
- continued questioning (repeating the question in another way or attaching a new question to an incomplete answer);
- mirroring (encouraging reflection by demonstrating the child's own activity or that of another child);
- problem variation (offering a different problem of the same degree of difficulty or a less difficult problem);
- offering assistance (providing the child with material, solving the problem together, and then having the child solve a similar problem, pre-structuring the solution strategy, drawing attention to errors and so on) (ibid.: 34).

Another area of development in the Netherlands has been to test children for whom Dutch is an additional language where an attempt has been made to ensure that language plays as small a part as possible. In the first example a bead problem is provided, and in each case the right of the page is free for making drawings or writing, as children wish (the 'scratch', or scrap paper) (see Figures 1.8 and 1.9).

Figure 1.8	scratch paper

Bead problem

A string of 20 beads. How many white beads are on this string?

___ white beads

Figure 1.9	scratch paper

Sweet problem

Three children are sharing 36 sweets

Here they are

How many sweets will each child get?

___ sweets

van den Heuvel-Panhuizen (1996:36)

Such developments in mathematics demand, on the one hand, teaching which stresses the use of contexts and models, children's own constructions and interactive approaches and, on the other hand, textbook development which shifts away from 'mechanical' problems to 'realistic' problems.

In summary, whatever the approach, it demands the use of sensitive assessment to investigate the child's informal knowledge and strategies as well as the formal knowledge constructed in different areas of mathematics in school, in different settings and over time. Furthermore, since differences in cultural and educational practices appear to underlie variations in rates of learning and levels of achievement, the adequacy of mathematics teaching should be considered so that the interaction between children's thinking and the educational context in which they are placed can be assessed.

Conclusion

International comparison suggests that current practices in our schools may place many of our children at risk of low achievement. Understanding, sensitively assessing and identifying, as well as teaching these children appropriately, including the smaller number of children with specific mathematical difficulties, requires a complex range of skills and is, hence, a particular challenge to the SENCO. This requires the consideration of:

- the close collaboration of the SENCO with senior management, mathematics and assessment co-ordinators;
- a whole-school audit of the mathematics curriculum and schemes of work, as well as of planning, teaching and assessment strategies;
- the provision of high-quality in-service training which includes modelling good lessons and effective, up-front interactive teaching;
- the dissemination of a truly developmental view of children's arithmetic, mental calculations and problem-solving strategies, which takes account both of informal knowledge and formal knowledge constructed in school and the influence of teaching on the rate and overall level of achievement.

References

Alexander, R., Rose, J. and Woodhead, C. (1992) *Curriculum Organisation and Classroom Practice in Primary Schools: A Discussion Paper*, London: HMSO.

Aubrey, C. (ed.) (1994) *The Role of Subject Knowledge in the Early Years of Schooling*, London: Falmer Press.

Aubrey, C., Tancig, S., Magajna, L. and Kavkler, M. (1998) 'Mathematics Lessons from Abroad', *Scientia Paedagogica Experimentalis*, xxxv, 1, 209–221.

Aubrey, C., Tancig, S., Magajna, L. and Kavkler, M. (2000) 'The Development of Numeracy in England and Slovenia', *Education 3–13*.

Basic Skills Agency (1998) *Family Numeracy Adds Up*, London: Basic Skills Agency.

Bierhoff, H. (1996) *Laying the Foundations of Numeracy: A Comparison of Primary Schools Textbooks in Britain, Germany and Switzerland*, London: National Institute of Economic and Social Research.

Bryant, B.R. and Rivera, D.P. (1997) 'Educational assessment of mathematical skills and abilities', *Journal of Learning Disabilities* 30: 57–68.

Department of Education (1993) *Education Act and Code of Practice*, London: HMSO.

Department for Education and Employment (DfEE) (1997a) *Excellence for All Children*, London: DfEE.

Department for Education and Employment (DfEE) (1997b) *Excellence in Schools*, London: DfEE.

Department for Education and Employment (DfEE) (1998a) *Teaching: High Status, High Standards, Requirements for Courses for Initial Teacher Training*, Circular 4/98, London: DfEE.

Department for Education and Employment (DfEE) (1998b) *The Implementation of the National Numeracy Strategy*, London: DfEE

Freudenthal, H. (1977) 'Response upon being awarded an honorary doctorate', *Euclides* 52: 336–8.

Fuson, K.C. and Kwon, Y. (1992) 'Korean children's single-digit addition and subtraction: numbers structured by ten', *Journal for Research in Mathematical Education* 23: 148–65.

Geary, D.C. (1990) 'A componential analysis of an early learning deficit', *Journal of Experimental Child Psychology* 49: 363–83.

Geary, D.C. (1993) 'Mathematical disabilities: cognitive, neurological and genetic components', *Psychological Bulletin* 114: 345–62.

Geary, D.C. (1994) *Children's Mathematical Development: Research and Practical Applications*, Washington, D.C.: American Psychological Association.

Geary, D.C., Widaman, K.F., Little, T.D. and Cormier, P. (1985) 'Cognitive "addition": comparison of learning disability and normally achieving elementary school children', *Cognitive Development* 2: 249–69.

Ginsburg, H.P. (1997) 'Mathematical learning disabilities: a view from developmental psychology', *Journal of Learning Disabilities* 30 (1): 20–33.

Ginsburg, H.P., Jacobs, S.F. and Lopez, L.S. (1993) 'Assessing mathematical thinking and learning potential', in R.B. Davis and C.S. Maher (eds), *Schools, Mathematics and the World of Reality*, Boston, Mass.: Allyn & Bacon, pp. 237–62.

Harris, S., Keys, W. and Fernandes, C. (1997) *Third International Mathematics and Science Study, Report on Nine-year-olds*, Slough: National Foundation for Educational Research.

Kavkler, M., Aubrey, C., Tancig, S., Magajna, L. (2000) 'Getting it Right from the Start? The Influence of Early School Entry on Later Achievement in Mathematics', *European Early Childhood Education Research Journal*, 8,1.

Merttens, R. (1997) 'Active ingredients', *The Times Educational Supplement: Primary and Pre-School*, 26 September, 11.

Ofsted (1999) *The National Numeracy Project, an HMI Evaluation*, London: Ofsted Publications

Schoenfeld, A.H. (1985) *Mathematical Problem-solving*, New York: Academic Press.

Strang, J.D. and Rourke, B.P. (1985) 'Arithmetic disability sub-types: the neuro-psychological significance of specific arithmetic impairment in children', in B.P. Rourke (ed.), *Neuropsychology of Learning Disabilities: Essentials of Sub-type Analysis*, New York: Guilford Press, pp.167–85.

Teacher Training Agency (TTA) (1997) *National Guidelines for the Special Educational Needs Coordinator*, London: TTA.

Teacher Training Agency (TTA) (1998) *National Professional Standards for Teachers and Headteachers*, London: TTA.

van den Heuvel-Panhuizen, M. (1996) *Assessment and Realistic Mathematics Education*, Utrecht: Freudenthal Institute, CDb Press.

van den Heuvel-Panhuizen, M. (1998) 'Realistic mathematics education: work in progress', NORMA proceedings, 5–9 June, Kristiansand, Norway.

Vygotskii, L.S. (1978) *Mind in Society: The Development of Higher Psychological Processes*, trans. M. Cole, Cambridge, Mass.: Harvard University Press.

Chapter 2
A sound beginning?

Introduction

CHAPTER 1 began by examining the rich informal mathematical knowledge young children develop outside school and outlined some of the strategies which could be devised to identify those in need of special teaching. This chapter – and subsequent ones – will consider the implications of adopting a developmental approach towards children's learning. This focuses on identifying the needs of children at the different stages of development in their counting, arithmetical calculation and problem-solving, in order to plan an active intervention to extend them. This approach is underpinned by a number of key principles:

- to assess accurately children's existing informal knowledge and strategies;
- to provide the appropriate experiences, activities and strategies, where necessary;
- to organise teaching which stimulates children's active construction of understanding;
- to relate teaching to what is known already; and
- to exploit everyday situations and a range of problem situations or contexts to introduce problem-solving and to foster the development of efficient strategies.

Accordingly, this chapter will draw upon the powerful and distinctive informal knowledge and active sense-making that children bring into school, which can form a foundation for later school learning. A sound knowledge of these early stages of mathematical learning can, in fact, be exploited very effectively to facilitate the development of those children who experience difficulties and delays in mathematical thinking and understanding. This chapter will also draw upon a long-term project which:

- over a number of years investigated children's early constructions of mathematics outside school; and
- identified what their class teachers made of this at school entry and throughout the children's first year in school.

The general principles described here are very compatible with the Dutch 'realistic' mathematical assessment practice introduced in Chapter 1. In fact, van den Heuvel-Panhuizen (1990) has developed group tasks for young children who have received no formal mathematical teaching, cannot read or write and have no experience of assessment. The key idea was to provide problems in contexts which young children could imagine (see Figure 2.1). The

Figure 2.1

Examples of the test items of the MORE grade 1 begin-test
van den Heuvel-Panhuizen (1994:26)

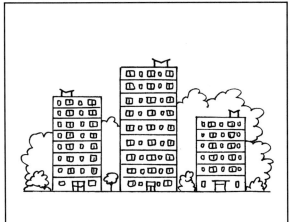

Relational concepts: mark the highest building.

Knowledge of symbols: mark the number 5.

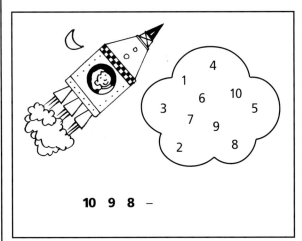

Counting sequence: next number?

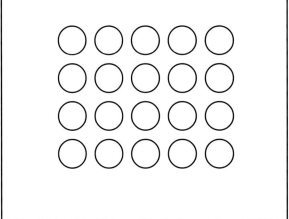

Resultative counting: colour 9 marbles.

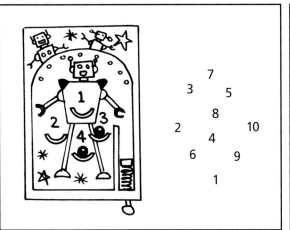

Addition in context (not-countable): how many points together?

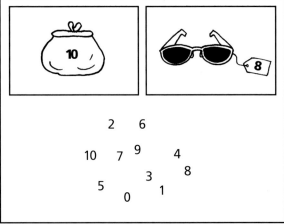

Subtraction in context (not-countable): how many pound coins left?

results showed that a large number of children were able to solve these tasks without help or supportive materials; moreover, a range of experts asked to predict the likely response considerably underestimated the knowledge and understanding of the young children concerned. If assessment is to influence teaching, children must be provided with the opportunity to demonstrate what they can do. It is very important, therefore, to use tests which are sensitive to their existing competence and which can access their different strategies.

Context

DfEE (1997), *Early Years Development Partnerships and Plans for 1998–9*, provided guidance to every local authority area on services integrating high-quality education and childcare for young children and their families. Plans must ensure that appropriate provision is available for children with special educational needs and providers must have regard to the Code of Practice in relation to the assessment and identification of special educational needs. Since both the *Desirable Outcomes for Children on Entering Compulsory Education* (1996) and *Baseline Assessment Scales* (1997) from SCAA (now the Qualifications and Curriculum Authority – QCA) cover aspects of language and literacy, mathematics, and personal and social development, the planning, teaching and assessment of children's early mathematical competence is now even more important in early childhood education for all providers. This is particularly the case now that a new foundation curriculum is being introduced by QCA (1999). In order for sensitive assessment and teaching to take place, however, it is essential that the available knowledge base concerning children's early learning of mathematics is more widely disseminated. Carpenter *et al.* (1989) found that workshops focusing entirely on children's mathematical thinking led to fundamental changes in teachers' beliefs and practices, and that these changes were reflected in six-year-old children's learning. Their work showed that providing new perspectives on children's thinking led to the development of new teaching contexts to support that development.

Chapter 1 outlined the quantitative environment in which young children grow up and the 'situated' knowledge that children construct in this context before formal schooling begins. This chapter describes:

- the major features of this knowledge;
- what learning and instruction takes place in the first year of schooling;
- the implications of this for the teaching of number, arithmetic and problem-solving to those who are not successful in the early stages of learning.

Accordingly, the next section concentrates on children's numerosity, or early discrimination of number, counting, arithmetic and problem-solving.

Numerosity

Research that has been carried out over the last quarter of a century has begun to map out the development of children's early numerical competence. Even very young children can:

- discriminate between small arrays of objects which differ by one;
- recognise that three objects is *more* than two or two is *less* than three (in other words, show some awareness of ordinality from an early age);
- add and subtract with small quantities.

The sensitivity of infants between four and twelve months to differences between two and three items has been demonstrated many times by different researchers under different conditions – whether stimuli are seen or heard, for instance, matching drum beats to photographs of objects (Starkey *et al.*, 1983; Moore *et al.*, 1987). Thus, even infants are believed to represent and to remember quantities of up to three or four. An innate pre-verbal counting or 'subitising' which allows infants to recognise the size of small quantities is not, however, an indication of sensitivity to ordinality, that is, the ranking or ordering of these representations.

Nevertheless, there is some indication that infants in the first eighteen months of life are beginning to distinguish 'more than' and 'less than'. Furthermore, infants as young as five months may be able to add and subtract small quantities. Wynn (1992) found that small infants stared longer at small arrays of Mickey Mouse dolls when changes they had seen the experimenter make to the array, by adding or subtracting a doll, were at variance with the manipulated arrangement displayed. These findings all point towards an innate sensitivity to quantity (Gallistel and Gelman, 1992), or numerosity; and an understanding of ordinal relationships for three to four items seems to emerge by around eighteen months of age.

Counting

Around the world, children of two years and above regularly take part in counting and number activities involving toys, food and body parts, often in the context of counting rhymes and jingles. Moreover, these naturally occurring activities link counting and number names to particular quantities, such as five to the little finger after the counting of the five fingers on one hand to represent 'Five currant buns in a baker's shop'.

The ability to understand counting and number concepts, whilst it begins early, probably develops over the period from two to eight years old. Most complex, perhaps, is the child's learning of counting principles, that is, a procedure for *enumerating* or assigning cardinal or ordinal meaning to objects being counted.

This requires children not only to memorise number words in a correct sequence but to map this on to their growing understanding of quantity and concepts of number. The basic skills or principles of counting have been investigated by many people (Fuson, 1988; Gelman and Gallistel, 1978; Wynn, 1990). A list of these with some suggestions for how they can be taught is shown in Figure 2.2.

Figure 2.2

Children need to know

- How to say the number sequence zero to ten, to twenty and beyond – counting rhymes such as 'One, two, three, four, five, once I caught a fish alive' and 'Ten green bottles' are fun.
- How to count on from a given number when it does not begin with one and how to say what number comes after/before another given number – whole-class questioning can be used: 'What number comes after three/before one?' 'Count on from four'.
- How to count back from a given number – from five to zero, from ten to zero, from twenty to zero – again, children enjoy counting rhymes such as 'Five currant buns in a baker's shop', or 'One man went to mow'.
- Some 'big' numbers in their environment: these may be in the hundreds or thousands or even millions – children already know familiar house numbers and telephone numbers and begin to recognise that these are part of the counting sequence: 'two hundred and one, two hundred and two . . . '
- How to count groups of objects reliably to five, to ten and beyond: in response to 'How many?' children can count objects in the home corner, pies in the sandpit, fingers, buttons, conkers, or matches of varying amounts, sizes and configurations. They can count a specified amount from packets, plates or jars.
- The size of arrays of up to six without counting (subitising): encourage children to:
    - count objects without touching them, showing small numbers on fingers;
    - count footsteps, claps and drumbeats;
    - count on board games and number tracks, forwards and backwards;
    - count in twos (odds and evens) and use jingles, such as 'Two, four, six, eight, ten' and a number track. Start by *whispering* the second number: 'one, *two*, three, *four*'; count in tens – zero, ten, twenty – to one hundred and back and know what number comes before and after.
- How to read numerals – pupils can read numbers on small/large cards, on calculators, on number lines and grids, on telephones and clock faces; they can match numerals to collections of objects and to dice spots.
- How to write numbers: let the children trace numbers in sand, in finger paint and on dot numerals. Make use of a number frieze. Use appropriate words to compare and order: bigger, smaller, larger, more, less, fewer, most, least and first, last, before, next, between and after.
- How to sequence a set of numbers, one to ten and ten to twenty, or say which numbers lie between two others: help children to put in order a set of number cards. Which is first/next/last? Fill in the missing numbers on the number line: 1, 2, 3 . . . 9, 10. Order the numbers 4, 3, 5, 1, 2. Use ordinal numbers with lines of cards, dolls, bricks, farm animals or queues of children to answer 'How many in front/behind?', 'Which is a third?' and so on.
- How to estimate: choose the most likely between two numbers, using words like 'nearly', 'close', 'about the same', 'too many' or 'too few' – ask questions like: 'Are there six or twenty six pencils in this jar?' 'How many pages in this book . . . about five, or about twenty?'
- How to use halves in a practical context, for instance, cutting a cake or a piece of string or relating to a birthday, such as 4° years.

Continued over

- How to use the vocabulary of addition and subtraction: 'more', 'add', 'sum', 'total', 'altogether', 'take away', 'subtract', 'how many left', 'difference between', 'how many', 'more', 'less'.
- How to add or subtract one – encourage role play, for example getting on and off a bus.
- Addition as combining two groups and three groups – say: 'Count out four sweets. Now count out three sweets. How many altogether?' or 'There are five cars in the garage. Four leave so how many are left?'
- That combining two groups – or three groups – is addition: 'Count three sweets and four sweets. How many altogether?' 'Show me three fingers on your right hand. Now show me two fingers on your left hand. How many altogether?'
- Addition as counting on: say 'There are three cards and four cards. How many altogether? Count on three from four.'
- 'Doubles' by counting on: use such questions as 'How many legs do two bears have?' 'How many wheels do two cars have?'
- How to find solutions to 'hidden number' problems: 'Count four teddies and put them in a covered basket. Put three more on the table. How many altogether?'
- How to separate a number of objects into two groups: 'Find different ways to separate ten jelly beans.' 'Bowl at six skittles. How many have fallen down?'
- How to combine two groups to make a given number: 'How many different towers of six bricks can be made in two different colours?'
- How to take away a small number from a larger one and count the remainder – use problems such as 'You have nine pennies and spend three. How many are left?'
- How to take away a small number from a larger one and count back from the larger number to find the remainder – say, for example, 'We made eight pizzas and you ate three. How many do we have left? Count back three from eight.'
- How to find out how many have been removed from a large group: count back to a number (or count up from a number) – try 'There were six eggs in this container and now there is only one. How many have gone?' ('Count up from one to six/ count down from six to one'.)
- How to find out how many more are needed to make a larger number – an example of this problem is: 'Ben has five sweets and Charlotte has two. How many more sweets does Ben have than Charlotte?'
- How to find the difference between two numbers by counting up or counting back – show this, for example, with apples: 'There are four apples in this bag and five apples in this one. What is the difference between the apples?'
- How to separate a number of objects into three groups – ask: 'Find different ways to put eight cakes on three plates (or eight beans on three saucers).'
- How to combine three groups to make a particular group size – help with such concrete problems as: 'Make towers of nine cubes with three different colours.'

Learning the counting principles is a difficult task and may not be complete in many four-year-olds or older children with learning difficulties. Normally somewhere between two and three years children begin to use number names when counting 'one, two, three . . .' In other words, they associate specific number 'tags' or words with mental representations of quantity and they use these in their counting activities. These skills require learning by rote the culture's number words up to and above ten, which is particularly difficult for English-speaking children, and, indeed for most European children, by comparison with Asian language-speaking pre-schoolers. Asian languages carry a one-to-one relationship between number words greater than ten reflecting the underlying ten-base system, so that eleven is 'ten one', twelve is 'ten two' and so on. The advantages are that there are fewer number words to memorise and the tens and units values are enshrined in the word. As a result English-speaking children take longer to learn the rote number sequence, the underlying base-ten principles and make more sequencing errors later in writing numbers, for example, confusing '71' with '17'. Gelman and Gallistel (1978) have suggested that counting objects involves:

- 'tagging' or assigning a number word to the counted items; and
- 'partitioning', which involves separating the items to be counted into two parts, those already counted and those which still need to be counted.

In the course of finger pointing (or making eye fixations, in the case of adults) co-ordination of tagging and partitioning frequently leads to errors of:

- either continuing to count after pointing to the last object; or
- saying more than one number tag whilst pointing to one object.

In the course of this activity, moreover, children are not simply learning that the number word assigned to the last counted object represents the total number of the counted objects (cardinality) but that successive number words represent larger quantities (ordinality). It is likely that in the context of responding to the question 'How many?', many three- to four-year-olds may correctly respond by repeating the last number tag without understanding cardinality. In this respect Piaget's (1965) classic experiments have shown how children confuse the number of objects in identical rows when one row is spread out. Children thus appear to recognise cardinality in some conditions but visual (perceptual) clues can disrupt this. Similarly, young children will commonly match items or use a non-numerical strategy when asked which of two sets of objects has more. This introduces a further important notion of 'equivalence' or the child's knowledge that two quantities are the 'same', 'greater than', 'less than' or 'not the same'. Many four- and five-year-old children will thus determine which of two sets has more or less by counting and comparing the cardinal values in each situation. It may be the case, however, that up to seven years children will continue to be confused by perceptual cues, such as length (or spread) of items to be counted.

Understanding of 'more than' and 'less than' is also demonstrated in young children's sharing of sweets or cakes among a group of friends or the family, where the goodies may be simply 'dumped' so that everyone gets some but no concern is shown to ensure that friends or family members receive equal numbers. The 'dumping' strategy may be supported by checking with the use of counting. Most older pre-school children or early school-aged children, however, will use 'distributive counting' – 'one for me, one for you' – or even share in groups of two or three items at a time. Again the same trends can be observed, from pre-quantitative strategies to determine equivalence or apportion shares, towards careful numerical procedures based on counting. Acquisition of counting skills in children, therefore, involves early innate, intuitive skills and essential experiences. Whatever the relative contribution of the two, young children and even infants develop very considerable competence.

How to assess what children know

Counting words

(adapted from Ginsburg and Russell, 1981; and Saxe, *et al.*, 1987)

Materials: puppet; 2 copies of a number sheet showing numbers 1–100

The purpose of this task is to determine how far children can recite the counting words in the conventional order.

1.I want you to count as high as you can for me for *(puppet's name)*.

Prompt: If there is no response from the child repeat 1 , adding '*1,2, 3 . . .*'

This task is repeated once, and the highest number the child achieves without making a mistake is used as a measure of the child's number words.

Record each trial on the number sheets. Tick each number stated in the correct order and circle omissions.

Of two trials, record the highest number the child achieves without getting the number order wrong. This is used as a measure of the child's rote counting. (Some four-year-olds can count to at least 100.) Write down in longhand any other noteworthy features.

1	2	3	4	5	6	7	8	9	10
11	12	13	14	15	16	17	18	19	20
21	22	23	24	25	26	27	28	29	30
31	32	33	34	35	36	37	38	39	40
41	42	43	44	45	46	47	48	49	50
51	52	53	54	55	56	57	58	59	60
61	62	63	64	65	66	67	68	69	70
71	72	73	74	75	76	77	78	79	80
81	82	83	84	85	86	87	88	89	90
91	92	93	94	95	96	97	98	99	100

Counting Objects within 10

(based on work of Gelman and Galhistel, 1978)

Materials: 12 identical objects (for example, small wooden horses) and puppet as before. Set out the horses as indicated.

1. (3 items in a line) Can you count these for me? (for *puppet's name*)

2. (3 items in a group) Can you count these for me? (for *puppet's name*)

3. (7 items in a line) Can you count these for me? (for *puppet's name*)

4. (7 items in a circle) Can you count these for me? (for *puppet's name*)

5. (12 items in a group) Can you give me 4 of the horses? (for *puppet's name*)

6. (12 items in a group) Can you give me 10 of the horses? (for *puppet's name*)

Record the numeral given for the count. Also record strategies: counting aloud or sub-vocally, pointing, touching, moving objects, head pointing, ability to stop at cardinal number at 4, 5, and 6. Write down in longhand any other noteworthy features. Tick and record the number of correct responses out of a possible 6.

Order invariance

(adapted from Baroody, 1979, Gelman and Gallistel, 1978 and Ginsburg and Russell, 1981)

Materials: wooden farm animals

Administer at two levels of set size: 4 and 6.

1. I want you to tell me how many animals there are. Let's count them starting with this one. *(Interviewer points to the animal on the child's extreme left and the child counts.)*

      4:

      6:

2. You've got 4/6 animals counting this way, from this end *(indicating the direction of the child's count)*. How many animals do you think there would be if you counted this way and made this animal number 1? *(Interviewer makes a motion to the animal on the child's extreme right.)*

      4.

      6:

3. How many do you think there would be if you made this one number 1 *(indicating the second item from the left in 4 and third from the left in 6)*?

      4:

      6:

The child is assigned a score of 1 for each correct judgement. Tick each correct response and note any interesting behaviour. Record the correct responses out of 6.

Reading Numbers

(based on a procedure from Baroody, 1979; Gelman and Gallistel, 1978; and Ginsburg and Russell,1981.)

Materials: puppet; pictures of everyday objects/people bearing numbers presented in the following sequence: 3, 4, 2, 1, 6, 5, 7, 10, 9, 8, 12, 15, 27

The purpose of this test is to assess children's ability to recognise written numerals:

1. I *(puppet's name)* would like to know what these numbers are. Would you please say them to me (him)? What is this number? *(Indicate number on first picture and so on.)*

3

4

2

1

6

5

7

10

9

8

8

12

15

27

Tick each correct response and note other responses made. Record the score, computed by counting the number of times the child produces the correct response.

Writing Numbers

(based on a procedure of Hughes, 1986)

Materials: 1 pad of paper; pencil; 10 bricks

The child is presented with a paper and pencil and a line of bricks and asked:

1 Can you put something on the paper to show how many bricks are on the table? Prompt: if there is no response from the child, add:

What could you put on the paper to show me how many bricks there are?

When something has been put on the paper the bricks are removed and a fresh piece of paper placed in front of the child.

The sequence for presenting the bricks is: 3, 4, 2, 1, 6, 5, 7, 10, 9, 8.

Remember to record on each sheet the number of bricks presented to the child. Note anything which the child says or does which is of interest.

Tick the correct response:

3

4

2

1

6

5

7

10

9

8

Record the score, computed by counting the number of the times the child produces the correct number for the picture presented.

Ordering numbers

(based on work of Carpenter, Fennema and Peterson, 1987)

Materials: puppet

1. Say: Tell me *(puppet's name)* what number comes after 39

2. What number comes after 6?

3. What number comes after 7?

4. What number comes after 4?

5. What number comes after 9?

6. What number comes after 2?

7. What number comes after 8?

8. What number comes after 1?

9. What number comes after 5?

10. What number comes after 10?

11. What number comes before 3?

12. What number comes before 6?

13. What number comes before 7?

14. What number comes before 4?

15. What number comes before 9?

16. What number comes before 2?

17. What number comes before 8?

18. What number comes before 1?

19. What number comes before 5?

20. What number comes before 10?

Tick correct responses, compute the total by counting the number of times the child produces the correct 'after' response and the correct 'before' response, each out of a possible 10.

Understands number operations of addition and subtraction

(adapted from Baroody, 1979, Ginsburg and Russell, 1981 and using the classification system of Carpenter, Fennema, Peterson and Carey, 1988)

Materials: puppet; coins.

1. Puppet wants to buy some ice cream so I gave him 3 pennies. But wait, he says now he really needs 4 pennies. Can you fix it so he really gets 4?

Repeat for following conditions:

2. $4 + \_ = 6$

3. $5 + \_ = 8$

4. $6 + \_ = 10$

5. $4 + \_ = 9$

6. Puppet wants to buy a bag of sweets, so I gave him 5 pence. But wait, he says he really only needs 4 pence. Can you fix it so he gets 4 pence?

Repeat for the following conditions:

7. $6 - \_ = 4$

8. $5 - \_ = 2$

9. $8 - \_ = 4$

10. $9 - \_ = 4$

Tick the correct responses and note any interesting comments or behaviour. Record the score, computed by counting the number of times the child produces the correct response to addition tasks and the number of times the child produces the correct response to subtraction tasks, with a total of 5 for each.

Division as sharing and multiplication as continuous addition

(adapted from Desforges and Desforges, 1980), with two items related to

Materials: 3 bears, sweets
   1. [4 sweets, 2 bears] *Say*: Can you share these sweets between these bears?
      Prompt (once): . . . so it's fair.

   2. [6 sweets, 3 bears] Can you share these sweets among these bears?
      Prompt (once): ... so it's fair.

   3. [9 sweets, 3 bears] Can you share these sweets among these bears?
      Prompt (once): . . . so it's fair.

   4. [5 sweets, 2 bears] Can you share these sweets between these bears?
      Prompt (once) : . . . so it's fair.

   5. If the child identifies that there is one over, ask: What can you do to make it
      fair to the bears?

Tick for correct sharing. Note strategies: dealing sweets out in ones or groups, method of dealing with remainders at 5 and any other noteworthy behaviour. Record correct responses out of 5.

Materials: do not draw attention to bears but leave on the table

   1. Say: How many legs have two teddies got?
      Prompt (once): One teddy has two legs, so

   2. How many legs have three teddies got?

Record replies and any noteworthy behaviour. Tick correct responses and record, out of possible 2.

Arithmetic and problem-solving

The previous section demonstrated clearly that young children, even infants perhaps, have a fundamental understanding that addition and subtraction influences quantity. In the early stages of development solving arithmetic problems depends heavily on counting and number knowledge of the culture's number system. Before schooling starts, however, there are strong similarities in children's arithmetic strategies. This, in itself, is unsurprising since at any one time children may well use a range – or mix – of different strategies, with a gradual shift towards those which are more flexible and efficient. As international studies reveal, different learning experiences in number and arithmetic, as well as the language differences noted earlier, influence the skills and strategies used. By the age of four years children begin to calculate in concrete addition situations. For instance, set the familiar task of adding a set of three sweets to another group of four sweets, children will generally manage this by:

- a 'counting all' strategy, counting each set separately – 1, 2, 3 . . . 1, 2, 3, 4, before counting 1, 2, 3, 4, 5, 6, 7 altogether. Fingers can be used to represent the number of objects and help children to keep track of the number sequence being counted. Faced with the simple written problem 4 + 3, without concrete objects, children will use fingers (four lifted on the left hand and three fingers lifted on the right hand). The child then moves each finger in succession as it is counted.

In time and even without formal instruction counting strategies mature and 'counting all' is gradually discarded in favour of 'counting on':

- counting on from the first number regardless of size – 1, 2, 3 . . . 4, 5, 6, 7; and then, finally,
- counting from the larger number . . . 5, 6, 7 . . . gradually takes over by six years as children find it is easier to count from the larger number. These two strategies suggest that the child recognises that the cardinal value of the first number is a short cut to the last.

Over time children move from finger counting to verbal counting. Five- and six-year-olds use both, and fingers support calculations with larger numbers.

As children gain experience with counting strategies they begin to recognise that numbers can be 'decomposed' or split into smaller numbers. This paves the way for learning number facts: 5 + 3 may, for instance, be recognised as the same as or equivalent to 4 + 4. 'Doubles' facts are often learned early.

Children's simple subtraction follows the same general pattern of development as addition. Early on, actual objects will be manipulated. Most five- and six-year-olds will still count to solve simple subtraction problems and, as with addition, this is done first with the aid of fingers to represent the numbers to be manipulated and to help keep track. With subtraction, however, this can involve counting either up or down.

Counting backwards and keeping track of the counting is hard. When using concrete materials children will separate the set to be removed and count the remaining objects; just as with finger-counting the number to be subtracted is represented by fingers folded down and the remaining fingers will be counted. To count down 8 – 3, for example, the child needs to lift eight fingers and then fold down three in succession whilst counting down – 7, 6, 5 – or count up – 1, 2, 3, 4, 5.

Meanwhile, four-year-olds usually regard addition and subtraction as the action of combining (change–join) or separating (change–separate) sets, acting on sets to create a new larger or smaller set (see Figure 2.3).

Figure 2.3

Ben had eight sweets but gave two to Jayne. How many are left?

Ben has three sweets. Jayne gave him four more. How many sweets are there altogether?

It is important to realise that the child does not typically regard this as the equivalence between two quantities. 3 + 4 is not regarded as the equivalent to 7 and, probably, neither is 3 + 4 seen as another way of expressing 4 + 3. It should be stressed that actions learned in one context do not automatically transfer to another setting without formal teaching.

The first year at school

Our own work with four-year-olds and their reception teachers showed not only that children brought into school a rich informal knowledge of counting, recognition of numerals, skill in simple addition, subtraction and social sharing, but that this matured considerably over the children's first year in school (Figure 2.4).

Figure 2.4

In children's rote counting:

- 11 could not recite the number sequence to 10 at the beginning of the year, only 1 by the end;
- 34 per cent could recite to 20 initially, 76 per cent by the end of the year;
- 12 per cent could recite well over 20 initially, 37 per cent by the end;
- 2 could recite to over 100 initially, 12 by the summer.
  (The range was as wide at the end of the year as at the beginning.)

In counting:

- 30 per cent counted to 10 reliably initially, 72 per cent by the summer;
- 42 per cent could not count to 10 reliably initially, 7 per cent by the end;
- 27 per cent were variable in counting skill to 10 initially, 10 per cent by the end.

In recognition of numerals:

- 33 per cent recognised the first ten numerals initially, 80 per cent by the end;
- 15 per cent could also read twelve and fifteen numerals initially, 50 per cent by the summer.

In writing numerals:

- 27 per cent wrote more than eight numerals initially, 75 per cent by the end.

In giving the number *after* or *before* a given number:

- 28 per cent managed more than eight 'number after' tasks initially, 64 per cent by the summer;
- 9 per cent managed more than eight 'number before' tasks initially, 30 per cent by the summer
  (43 per cent still found this task difficult – they scored less than 3 – in the summer).

In operations:

- 18 per cent solved five addition problems initially, 43 per cent by the end; 9 per cent still could not solve any by the summer;
- 46 per cent solved five subtraction problems initially, 86 per cent by the end.

In distributive counting (sharing with remainders):

- 63 per cent solved five simple problems initially, 84 per cent by the end.

In 'doubles' facts (legs of teddies × 2 and × 3):

- 21 per cent answered two problems correctly initially, 40 per cent by the end;
- 48 per cent did not understand the task intially, 43 per cent by the end.

Most striking was the sheer range of knowledge and abilities possessed by children at the beginning of schooling; indeed, the diversity of this knowledge was in no way diminished by the end of the year. Some were counting reliably, recognising numerals, able to solve simple addition and subtraction problems on entry, as well as carry out distributive counting tasks. Improvement in others was observed in counting reliably, reading and writing numbers and problem-solving. A few others still showed little knowledge of counting, number skills or arithmetic by the end of the year. In almost all tasks set, however, it was significant that those children with low scores started in January; thus they received less formal teaching and were both younger and less mature. The characteristics of the observed curriculum are summarised in Figure 2.5.

Figure 2.5

Characteristics of the observed curriculum

- play, flexibility and choice to explore independently sand, water and construction toys with an additional teacher-focus group;
- some use of card and board number games;
- sorting, matching, classifying and sets (with no evidence that children saw the connection between this and other number activities);
- much emphasis on choral counting and one-to-one correspondence (as a class and in groups) but
    - most emphasis on numbers to 10
    - some attention to 'teens'
    - occasional focus on twenties (in practice children had most difficulty in co-ordinating the sequence of number names with objects, usually pointing);
- notable absence of simple problem-solving involving calculation (addition, subtraction) with small numbers.

In spite of the fact that many children entered school with competence in solving simple concrete word problems, the introduction of calculation in school was determined by its position in the published school scheme being used. In fact, of seven teachers observed in one year of the project, four were not observed to introduce any simple calculation. Of the other three teachers, three lessons out of eighteen involved simple calculation for one; for a second teacher, two lessons out of nineteen; and a third, one lesson out of thirteen. Overall there was little evidence of four-year-olds carrying out addition and subtraction in simple, problem-solving situations. This finding mirrors children's home experience, discussed above, where parents are not observed to carry out simple problem-solving and sums. Furthermore, whilst nearly half of the children could count to well over 20 when they entered school, in most classrooms counting activities focused on numbers up to 10. Great emphasis was placed on reading, writing and counting objects within 10 and children developed competence in these areas. Whilst choral counting took place, there was little emphasis on the development of children's oral mental methods of calculation.

Implications for teaching

How do children learn and what can we do as teachers? The principles that can be derived from a developmental approach are summarised in Figure 2.6.

In conclusion, there is more to counting than the rote counting of number names and the one-to-one correspondence between these number names and the objects being counted. Many children do not find this easy. Sometimes, they use a partitioning board which allows counted items to be physically moved into

Figure 2.6

The principles of a 'developmental' approach

To teach number in the early years it is important to:

- assess the informal knowledge and strategies children already have;
- use the 'clinical interview' technique of non-standard, flexible questioning (and 'talkaloud' strategies if needed);
- provide early quantitative experience if necessary;
- relate teaching to what is known already;
- focus on active construction and discussion;
- encourage children to use objects, to draw pictures and tallies to represent their numerical/ quantitative ideas *and* to talk about these;
- use teaching to develop understanding of problem-solving as the organising focus (numerical activities should always have a purpose);
- use small numbers for calculation but at the same time extend children's counting skills with larger numbers (up to 20 and beyond);
- foster the development of more efficient counting strategies;
- focus on patterns and relationships between numbers and mastery of simple combinations (counting up and down, 'number after' rule: 2 +1, 1+ 1; 'skip next number': 2, 4);
- introduce symbolic arithmetic with a flip chart (or chalkboard) linked to oral methods;
- stimulate counting, reasoning and recall to master basic numbers;
- when symbolic arithmetic is introduced, link to concrete models and situations (in other words, reverse the process: symbol back to model situation that it represents);
- make sure that simple addition/subtraction problems are introduced in various ways: as well as 'join–change' and 'separate–change' problems, introduce 'difference' and 'equalise', for instance, using a balance bar.

a different section of the board; this helps children to separate and, hence, keep track of counted items. Similarly, there is more to problem-solving than simple change–join and change–separate problems.

Children need to be introduced to different problem types which require them to *compare* two quantities and calculate the difference or to *equalise* two quantities to determine what must be added to one to make both quantities the same. This helps to develop flexibility in thinking about number strategies and extends children's understanding of problem 'texts'.

If choral counting is already going on in classrooms, then this can be extended to numbers within 20, and beyond, with counting forwards and counting backwards and even 'skip' counting – 2, 4, 6, 8; 1, 3, 5, 7 – and so on. Simple mental calculation can also be introduced in class activities: 'If teddy has two toffees and one chocolate, how many sweeties does he have altogether?' King-size number cards can also be introduced to help children learn to recognise numerals and to practise number sequencing as a whole class as well as individually with their own small sets.

Using an argumentative puppet who makes deliberate mistakes in counting, ordering numbers and simple calculation, with orally-presented and recorded numbers, helps children to start talking about and pinpointing errors as well as considering alternative solution strategies.

Traditional card, board and playground games all provide valuable counting experience and, with teacher support, can help to develop understanding of ordinal numbers and calculation. (Who is going to be first/second/third? How many more do you need to finish?)

In order to build successfully on children's home learning experiences, teachers need to:

- develop awareness of the teaching potential of existing practical contexts and recognise that early care-givers use on-going practical activities to highlight number/mathematics as well as plan deliberately and teach didactically purposeful tasks related to number/mathematics;
- exploit existing activities in the home and outside the home for opportunities which involve counting, comparing, sorting, describing position, size and quantity;
- remain alert to the areas of children's early competence that mothers and early educators have tended to overlook: subitising (children's instant recognition of small groups or quantities) and simple real-life number problem-solving;
- note that although children's environment is rich in opportunity for number/mathematical experiences in terms of books, action rhymes and jingles, television programmes, play materials and contexts, indoors and outside, as well as more formal board and card games, these need an adult to support, demonstrate or model, coach and encourage children;
- and finally, in order to know what to do next, observe and question children whilst they are engaged in these activities (see the assessment tasks at the end of this chapter for illustration material).

In summary, the adult will need to intervene actively in order to:

- supply mathematical language: one, two, three, same, different, zero, more, less, fewer, bigger, smaller, longer, shorter, full, empty, square, circle, rectangle, triangle, 2D, cube, cuboid, sphere, pyramid, cone, 3D, under, over, forwards, backwards, before, after, corner, angle; as well as questions such as how many?, how many more/less/altogether?, and commands such as count, take away, add to, share;
- assess what children can do and understand and need to know next: Do they know some number words and can they recite them in an order? Can they say what comes before/after a given number? Can they co-ordinate their counting with pointing at objects in different arrangements? Do they really know that the last number in the count represents the size of the set or group of objects? Can they estimate/recognise the size of a small set of objects (for example, spots on a die or playing card) and check with

counting?

- introduce numerals: Do they recognise particular numerals (their own/ siblings' age, house number, shoe size, numbers on a clock and so on)? Can they match numerals to a group of objects? Can they begin to order wooden/plastic numerals to the known counting sequence? Can they select the right numeral to match a quantity in a board game, for example?
- decide how to introduce: patterns in number (recurring 1s, 2s, 3s, odds and evens, 1, 3, 5, and 2, 4, 6); comparing two sets/quantities (more, less, same? check by counting? match to see what is left over?); combining (putting together), separating (taking away) in the context of real-life problems; drawing attention to repeated combining (teddies' legs, cars' wheels, and so on); introducing simple fractions of a half and quarter in the context of cutting up cakes and sharing fruit.

We now know a great deal about the way children learn early counting, arithmetic and problem-solving. The challenge is to make use of a truly developmental approach to investigate their individual differences in knowledge and strategy use in order to ensure that our teaching both connects with and extends children's existing competence.

Figure 2.7

Things to note if there is a classroom assistant working with the a group

- The importance of children talking aloud about what they are doing.
- The need to encourage talk by questioning.
- The need to listen and probe further: Can you say more about that? What do you mean? Did anyone else do it another way? Can you say which was the easiest?
- The importance of asking questions: closed questions (What is the answer?) and open questions (What does that mean? How did you work that out?)
- The need to model the use of mathematical vocabulary (add, total, sum, take away, subtract, difference, figure, number, numeral, more/less than, how many, altogether, count on/ back – in twos, fives, tens).
- The importance of children explaining to each other and listening to one another's strategies.
- The need to encourage children to show on paper/OHP/chalkboard how they have worked out a problem.
- The importance of giving feedback to children and the class teacher on progress and achievements.
- The need to observe closely as well as listen to children talking about their ideas and recording their strategies and solutions.
- The importance of planning before the lesson:
  - the activity (what you/they will do)
  - the resources (what you/they will need to use)
  - key objectives (learning points/targets: what you/they learn)
  - recording during and after the lesson: this includes asking the children what they have learned, what they still need to learn, and what would help/make it easier to learn. It may also involve children with special needs, such as those with English as an additional language, specific learning difficulties or physical disabilities.

Figure 2.8

What might a numeracy lesson for five-year olds look like?

Finding out how many more by counting on

Objectives

- counting forwards and backwards 0–10;
- introducing simple word problems;
- using language: more than, less than, fewer than, how many, same.

Context
Young Dutch children solve practical problems in specific contexts. Early additon and subtraction is built around 'The Bus'. Children play mathematics drama and illustrative scenes about getting on and off a bus. Sums are presented in drawings of buses linked by arrows which indicate the direction and carry a sign showing how many people got on or off. The number is written on the side and the bus is faded out as the meaning of the symbols is learned.

Resources

- OHP transparencies of 'Wiskobus' and train
- five rows of pairs of chairs for a pretend bus
- sets of number cards: 0–5 and 0–10
- sets of train and bus cards 0–10

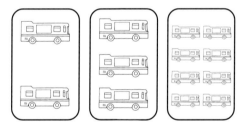

Introduction Choral counting on and back (10 minutes)

- Start by counting forwards and backwards: to 5, to 10 and back.
- Then 'one more' and 'one less' with numbers to 10 – children should model these with their fingers.
- Finally, try 'two more' and 'three more', and 'two less' and 'three less'.

Move to the pretend bus, where children model the problems: Four on the bus, then two more get on, now there are six. Seven on the bus, three get off, now there are four, and so on.

Development Main activity (20 minutes)
Children work in pairs. Teacher presents a bus problem on the OHP: 'There are two people on the bus. When it stops, three more get on. How many are there on the bus now?'

| 2 | +3 | ? |

Children work their own examples in pairs with sets of cards 0–5, 0–10 shown as numbers or as buses. Child 1 'reads' the number on the first card, which represents the people on the bus. Child 2 'reads' the next card, which represents people who got on the bus at the next stop. Together they work out how many passengers there are on the bus altogether. A lower-achieving group may need more practice with the pretend bus and oral methods.

Plenary Whole class (10 minutes)
Teacher presents simple 'train' problems on OHP.

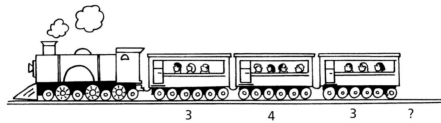

           3   4   3   ?

Ideas for class and individual work
Source: Boswinkel *et al.* (1996)

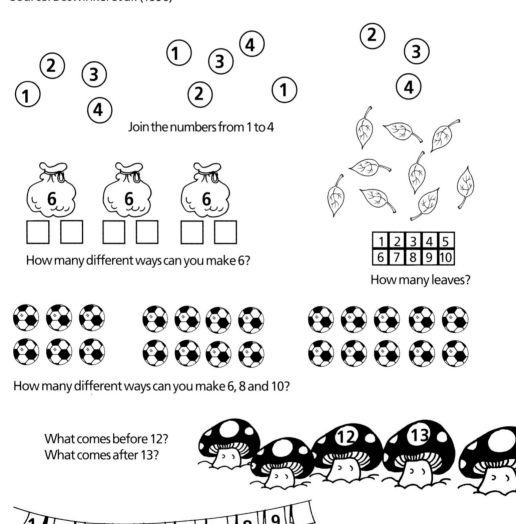

Join the numbers from 1 to 4

How many different ways can you make 6?

How many leaves?

How many different ways can you make 6, 8 and 10?

What comes before 12?
What comes after 13?

What are the missing numbers?

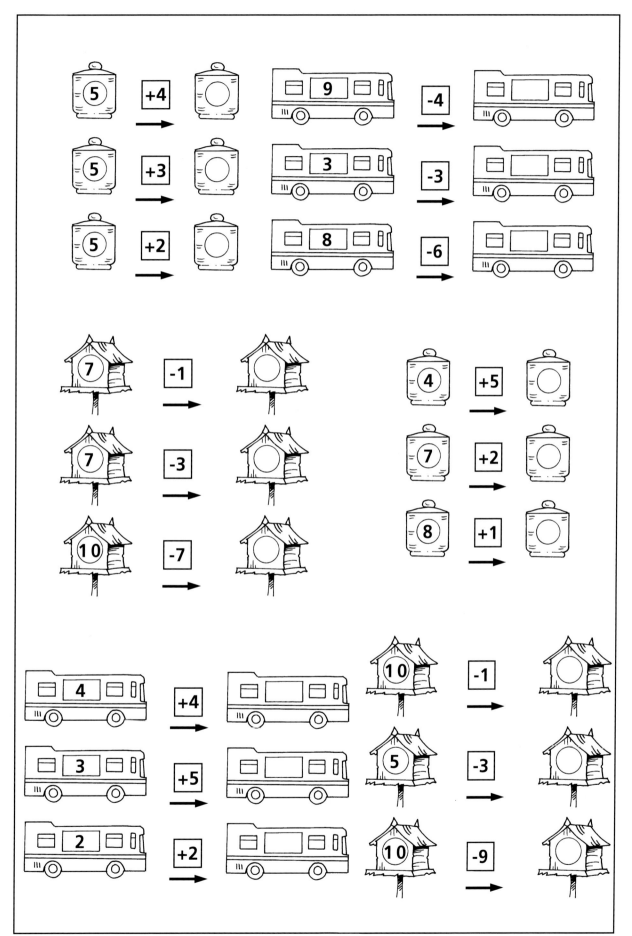

Source: Boswinkel *et al.* (1996)

Commentary

At this stage children are developing counting skills and building up number facts: 0–5, 5–10 and, later, 0–20. At the same time, they can also use an arithmetic rack as an ordinal (first, second, third . . .) and cardinal model.

This can be used for arithmetic to 10 as well as to 20. Its strength lies in its emphasis on the five-structure and its potential for illustrating 'doubles' facts, such as 2 and 2, or 4 and 4.

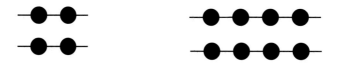

The possibility of moving beads at either end shows that the result stays the same. Taking 9 as an example:

Nine beads can be split into 6 + 3 and show that 3 + 6 gives the same answer (commutative property). The same nine beads can also be used to show that 9 – 6 = 3 is the same as 3 + 6 = 9 (inverse relation).

The double-decker bus representation is also used to illustrate properties:

and connections between 'doubles' and near-doubles:

Whilst children are using real-life problems, they are also being inducted into the logical properties of number.

Figure 2.9

Parent numeracy projects

The SENCO may wish to support parents in encouraging numeracy at home, in order to provide a sound start for four- to five-year-olds who may be at risk of under-achievement. Such support could include:

- comparing, sorting and matching;
- counting and recognising numbers;
- solving simple practical real-life problems;
- exploring shape and space.

The Basic Skills Agency (1998: 25) has shown that involvement in a Family Numeracy Project can be very effective in increasing numeracy-related home activities, which could include:

- sorting items of clothes, shopping and so in in order of size;
- looking at shapes in the street;
- looking at prices in the shops;
- looking at numbers in the street;
- looking at calendars;
- counting out items of shopping, toys and so on;
- playing games involving numbers and matching;
- looking at number/telling-the-time books;
- sorting items of shopping, toys and so on according to weight;
- cooking (weighing out ingredients);
- sorting clothes, shopping and so in into groups;
- matching items of clothing, toys and so on;
- singing number songs;
- playing computer games involving numbers;
- filling and emptying containers of different sizes;
- playing clapping games;
- playing with construction kits and building blocks.

The Basic Skills Agency supported fourteen local authority pilot projects which combined courses for parents with poor numeracy and for their children. What worked best was a three-strand programme lasting no more than twelve weeks and comprising a minimum of one-hour weekly joint sessions, two hours per week for parents alone and $1\frac{1}{2}$ hours per week for children. The courses included:

- challenging numeracy objectives for parents on accredited programmes;
- planned and explicit links between different strands of provision;
- content drawn from the Desirable Outcomes for Learning or the Early Years National Framework and the National Curriculum in both the children's and the joint sessions.

Figure 2.10   **How many people on the bus**

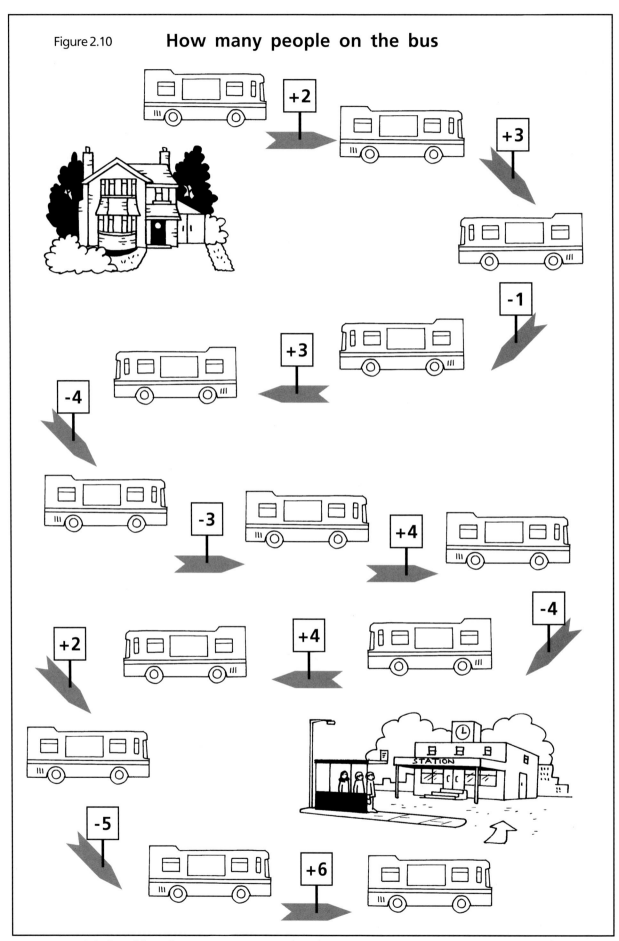

Source: Boswinkel *et al.* (1996)

Figure 2.11 **Different ways to make 4,7 and 10**

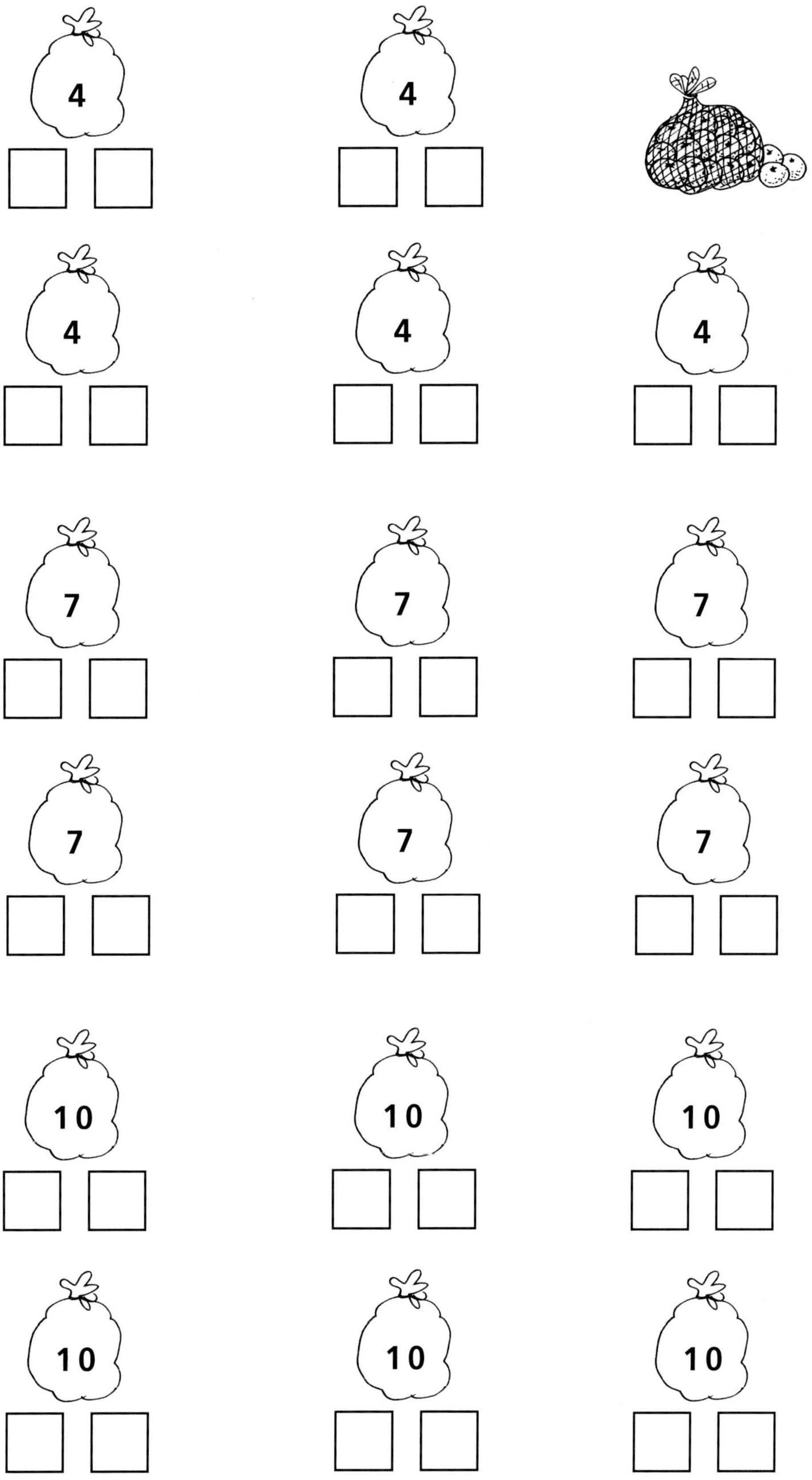

Source: Boswinkel *et al.* (1996)

Figure 2.12

Nine soldiers altogether . . . how many in each carriage?

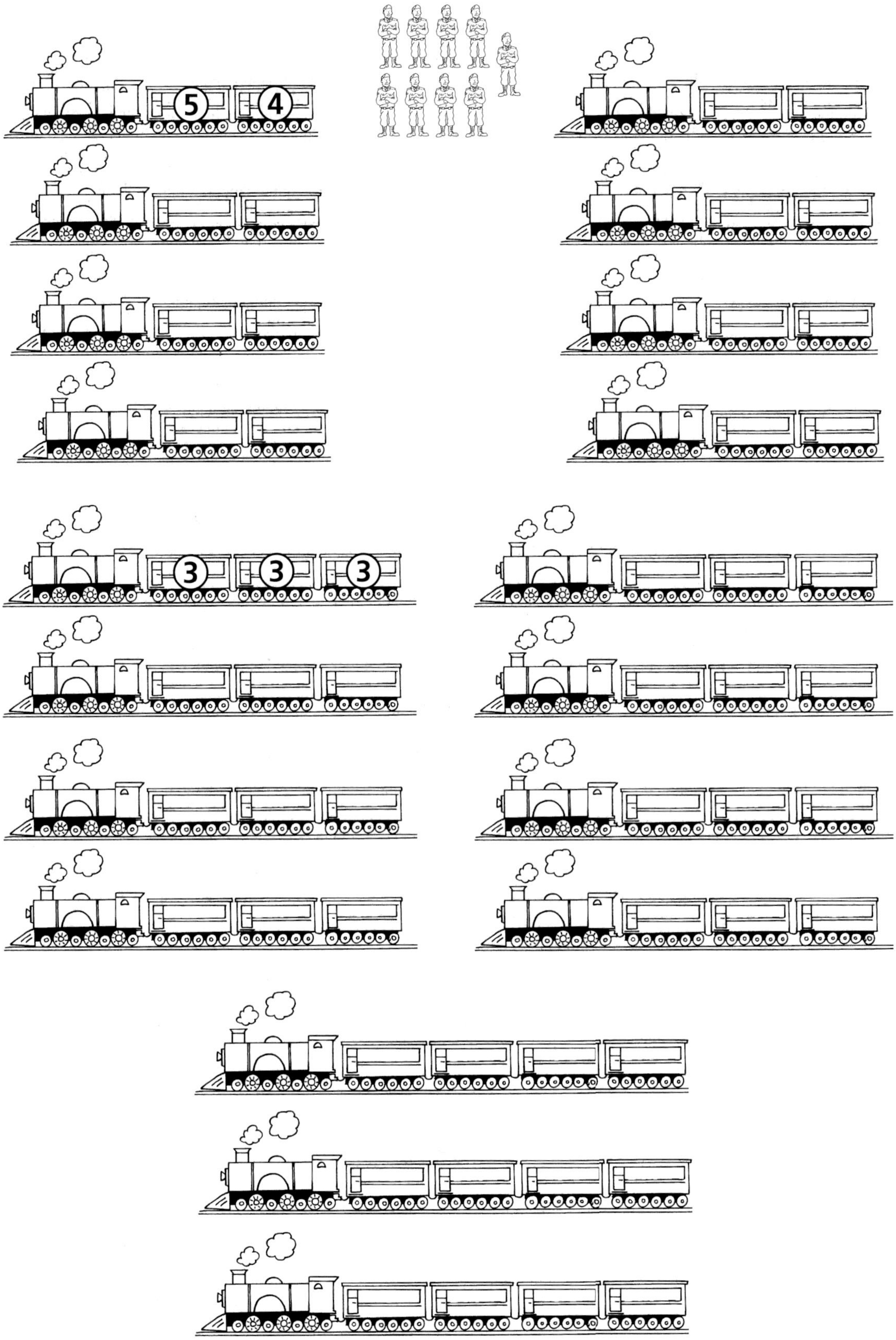

Source: Boswinkel *et al.* (1996)

References

Aubrey, C. (1997) *Mathematics Teaching in the Early Years: An Investigation of Teachers' Subject Knowledge*, London: Falmer Press.

Aubrey, C., Godfrey, R. and Godfrey, J. (1999) 'Children's early number experience in the home', paper presented to the Third Warwick International Early Years Conference, 12–16 April.

Baroody, J.A. (1979) 'The relationship among the development of counting, numerosity, conservation and basic arithmetic abilities', unpublished PhD thesis, Cornell University.

Basic Skills Agency with NFER (1998) *Family Numeracy Adds Up: Lessons from the Family Numeracy Pilot Programme*, London: Basic Skills Agency.

Boswinkel, N. *et al.* (1996) *Wis en Reken*, Werkboek 2, Groep 3, Utrecht: Uitgeverij Bekadidact.

Carpenter, T.P., Fennema, E. and Peterson, P.L. (1987) 'Teachers pedagogical content knowledge in mathematics', paper presented at the Annual Meeting of the American Educational Research Association, Washington D.C.

Carpenter, T.P., Fennema, E. and Peterson, P.L. (1989) 'Teachers pedagogical content belief in mathematics', *Cognition and Instruction*, 6,1, pp1–40.

Department for Education and Employment (DfEE) (1997) *Early Years Development: Partnerships and Plans for 1998–9*, London: DfEE.

Desforges, A. and Desforges, C. (1980) 'Number-based strategies of sharing in young children', *Educational Studies*, 6, 2, pp97–109

Fuson, K. (1988) *Children's Counting and Concepts of Number*, New York: Springer-Verlag.

Gallistel, C.R. and Gelman, R. (1992) 'Preverbal and verbal counting and computation', *Cognition* 44: 43–74.

Gelman, R. and Gallistel, C.R. (1978) *The Child's Understanding of Number*, Cambridge, Mass.: Harvard University Press.

Ginsburg, H.P. and Russell, R.L (1981) 'Social class and and racial influence on early mathematical thinking', monograph of the Society for Research in Child Development, 46, 6 serial no.193.

Hughes, M. (1986) *Children and Learning Difficulties in Learning Mathematics*, Oxford: Blackwell.

Moore, D., Benenson, J., Reznick, J. S., Peterson, M. and Kagan, J. (1987) 'Effect of auditory numerical information on infants' looking behaviour: contradictory evidence', *Developmental Psychology* 23: 665–70.

Piaget, J. (1965) *The Child's Conception of Number*, New York: W.W. Norton.

Saxe, G.B., Guberman, S.R. and Gearhart, M. (1987) 'Social processes in early mathematical development', monograph of the Society for Research in Child Development, 52, 2 serial no.216.

School Curriculum and Assessment Authority (SCAA) (1996) *Desirable Outcomes for Children on Entering Compulsory Education*, London: SCAA.

School Curriculum and Assessment Authority (SCAA) (1997) *Baseline Assessment Scales*, London: SCAA.

Starkey, P., Spelke, E.S. and Gelman, R. (1983) 'Detection of intermodel numerical correspondences by human infants', *Science* 222: 179–81.

Suggate, J. , Aubrey, C. and Pettitt, D. (1997) 'Children's mathematical knowledge in the first year of school', *European Early Childhood Education Research Journal*, 5 (2): 85–101.

van den Heuvel-Panhuizen, M. (1990) 'Realistic Arithmetical Mathematics Instruction and Tests', in K.P.E. Gravemejer, van den Heuvel-Panhuizen, M. and L. Streetland, *Context, Free Productions, Tests and Geometry in Realistic Mathematics Education*, Utrecht: Freudenthal Institute.

van den Heuvel-Panhuizen, M. (1996) *Assessment and Realistic Mathematics Education*, Utrecht: CD-β Press

Wynn, K. (1990) 'Children's understanding of counting', *Cognition* 36: 155–93.

Wynn, K. (1992) 'Addition and subtraction in human infants', *Nature* 358: 749–50.

Chapter 3

All sixes and sevens?

Introduction

The first chapter of this book showed how both previous and present governments have striven to set in place a wide range of policies to drive up standards of achievement in literacy and numeracy for pre-school and school-age children. These policies have fallen, according to the DfEE (1997), into three broad groups:

- policies to identify and meet all pupils' needs;
- policies to improve the quality of teaching through the introduction of new requirements for courses of initial teacher training (DfEE, 1998) and the national literacy and numeracy strategies;
- policies to challenge current standards and promote school performance through the publication of school performance tables and regular school inspections.

The first of these – identifying and meeting all pupils' needs – to 'get it right first time [by] giving young children a solid grounding in basic skills from the start to reduce the need for later remedial action' (DfEE, 1997) was the theme of the second chapter. The goal to 'ensure that, for the first time, pre-school children will work towards common (desirable) learning outcomes (including mathematics, language and literacy) for school entry at 5', however, is beginning to be questioned. Moreover, the aims of baseline assessment, focusing on early literacy and numeracy of all children at school entry 'to help teachers to understand their pupils' needs, provide valuable information to guide schools' targeting of resources and give a baseline for measuring future improvement' in national curriculum terms are, similarly, being critically evaluated. QCA (1999) is now proposing a foundation curriculum for three years to the end of the reception year, with early learning goals (instead of the current age-related Desirable Learning Outcomes).

The second chapter demonstrated how, in the early years of schooling, the focus is on activity and oral-mental methods. In the past there has been too much emphasis on reading and writing numbers and on written equations. In many schools these were carried out without monitoring children's understanding, and without teachers linking new work to children's existing numerical knowledge and calculation strategies. There was a danger that written, symbolic arithmetic was insufficiently linked to concrete models and situations or extended through the learning of number combinations and pattern relationships of numbers. Working with numbers within 10, then within 20 and, finally, within 100 and the teaching of more efficient strategies, so important for six- and seven-year-olds, is the focus of this chapter. In fact, our own comparative work in collaboration with the University of Ljubljana in Slovenia showed that whilst English six-year-olds have significantly higher scores than Slovene pre-schoolers for arithmetic and problem-solving tasks, by seven years – when Slovene children had been in school for only eight months – there was no significant difference in arithmetic skills between English and Slovene pupils. In other words, by seven years, the effects of an additional two years of formal schooling are negligible in comparison with a central European system which stresses preparation for formal schooling and with a tradition of relying entirely on oral methods of calculation until basic number facts and reliable calculation strategies have been established.

Context

The controversial Channel 4 programme *Dispatches* (29 January 1998) highlighted research funded by the Gatsby Foundation which claims that British children do less well at literacy and numeracy because they start formal schooling too early. In countries where children spend their earlier years *preparing* for school at six or seven years old, the socio-economic and developmental variations found in young children – whether physical, social-emotional, cognitive or language-related – are actually reduced (Nagy, 1989). Nagy's work, which brings together over twenty years of research, has demonstrated that children with a calendar age of six years can vary by up to three years in developmental terms. By this age it is already too late to address those developmental differences either by direct instruction at the time or by later schooling. The continental systems of pre-school preparation focus on the development of:

- the capacity to participate in an oral-linguistic approach to teaching;
- the appropriate co-operative group behaviour;
- conceptual understanding of the concepts of quantity, time, size and space which underlie later maths understanding.

These views support the developmental approach advocated in this book which emphasises the need for:

- sensitive assessment of what children know already about their quantitative world in terms of counting, arithmetic and problem-solving;
- recognition that there will be wide variations in the rates of learning and levels of mathematical achievement which teachers need to address;
- appreciation that international comparison suggests our current practices may place at risk of low achievement a high proportion of children in the early stages through too little emphasis on children talking aloud about and using their existing, informal counting and arithmetic strategies, too little emphasis on teaching of methods of calculation and too much emphasis on written exercises.

How do six- and seven-year-olds develop knowledge and understanding of number?

Whether six- and seven-year olds are following the numeracy framework, as English children do, or are entering formal schooling at six or seven years, as is sometimes the case in central Europe, surprisingly there is little disagreement about what must be achieved by the end of the school year. By the end of year 2 (year 1):

- in terms of counting and properties of number, children need to:
  - recite in order the number names to at least 100 (20) and back to zero;
  - count at least 100 (20) objects, regardless of arrangement;
  - count on and back in steps of 10 (1 for any small number) from any one- or two-digit number and back to zero;
  - count in twos from (zero, then one) any small number and recognise odd and even numbers to at least 30 (to about 20);
  - begin to county in steps of 3, 4 or 5 from zero, then from any small number to at least 30 (20 or more) and then back again;
  - begin to recognise multiples of 2, 5 or 10.

- in terms of place value and ordering, children need to:
  - read and write numbers to at least 100 (20);
  - know (begin to know) what each digit in a two-digit number represents and (partition a 'teens' number and begin to) partition a two-digit number into tens and ones (TU);
  - say the number that is 1 or 10 more or less than any given two-digit number (number to 20 or more);
  - understand and use the vocabulary of comparing and ordering numbers, including ordinal numbers to at least 100 (20);
  - compare two familiar numbers or measures, say which is more or less and give a number or measure which lies between them;
  - order a set of familiar numbers or measures.

- in terms of addition and subtraction calculation, children need to:
  - understand the operations of addition and related vocabulary, recognise that addition can be done in any order and understand that more than two numbers can be added together;
  - understand the operation of subtraction and related vocabulary;
  - understand the relationship between addition and subtraction.

- in terms of instant recall of addition/subtraction facts, children need to:
  - know by heart addition and subtraction facts for all numbers to at least 10 (5); addition 'doubles' for all numbers to 10, for example 8 + 8 (to at least 5; for example, 3 + 3); pairs of numbers with a total of 20, for

example, 13 + 7 or 16 + 4 (with a total of 10, for example, 3 + 7).

● in terms of mental calculation strategies, children need to:
  – put the larger number first;
  – count on and back in repeated steps of 10 or 2 (in ones, including 10;
    for example, 7 + 5);
  – identify near-doubles, using doubles already known, for example, 5 + 6 =
    11, using knowledge that 5 + 5 = 10;
  – partition (begin to) into 5 and a bit when adding 6, 7, 8 or 9, or into tens
    and units, and recombine;
  – use patterns of similar calculations, for example, 10 – 0 = 10, 10 – 1 = 9,
    10 – 2 = 8;
  – add/subtract 9 or 11 by adding/subtracting 10, then adjusting by 1;
  – add (begin to) three or four small numbers by putting the largest
    number first and/or finding pairs that make 10;
  – use the relationship between addition and subtraction;
  – use knowledge of number facts and place value to add/subtract a pair of
    numbers mentally within the range of 0 to 10, then 0 to at least 20,
    and then above;
  – bridge (begin to) through 10 or 20 and adjust when adding single-digit
    numbers; for example, 8 + 5 = 10 + 3, 18 + 5 = 20 + 3.

● in terms of multiplication and division, children need to:
  – understand (begin to) the operation of multiplication and the
    associated vocabulary;
  – understand (begin to) that multiplication can be done in any order;
  – understand (begin to) the operation of division and the associated
    vocabulary.

● for seven-year-olds only, they need to:
  – begin to understand the idea of a remainder;
  – make sensible decisions about rounding up or down after division;
  – understand the relationship between multiplication and division.

● in terms of instant recall of multiplication/division facts, children need to:
  – begin to know doubles of numbers to 10, and the corresponding halves.

● seven-year-olds need to:
  – know by heart doubles of all numbers to 10, doubles of multiples of 10
    to at least 50, and the corresponding halves;
  – know by heart multiplication and division facts for the 2 and 10 times
    table;
  – begin to know the multiplication and division facts for the 5 times table;
  – use the relationship between multiplication and division;
  – use knowledge of the number system and number facts to multiply or
    divide by 2, 5 or 10.

- for English pupils, more emphasis will be placed on checking that the results of calculations are reasonable. They need to:
  - check with the inverse operation;
  - repeat addition in a different order or by multiplication in the case of seven-year-olds;
  - check with an equivalent calculation;
  - check the effect of an operation;
  - approximate by rounding to the nearest 10;
  - give sensible estimates to about 100 objects.

- also for English pupils, in terms of decimals and fractions, they need to:
  - recognise and use in practical contexts simpe fractions, such as halves, quarters and thirds;
  - recognise the equivalence between two fractions; for example, two quarters = one half, two halves = one whole;
  - order two familiar fractions.

Also involved would be making decisions about appropriate number operations for problem-solving; solving number problems; recognising simple patterns, investigating statements about number by providing examples, explaining methods and strategies; using the four operations to solve real-life money problems and problems involving measures, as well as handling and interpreting numerical data presented in Venn or Carroll diagrams (two criteria), block graphs and simple tables (from the National Numeracy Project).

Our research showed that by the end of the first year in school most children have already learned the number sequence and can reliably count, and join and separate groups of objects to extend their knowledge of quantity and cardinality as well. By four to five years children have begun to count and calculate in concrete activities. In fact, for solving simple addition such as 4 + 3 children use a number of distinct strategies:

- concrete aids, manipulatives, or the actual objects being counted;
- finger counting;
- verbal counting without the concrete materials;
- derived fact strategies;
- fact retrieval.

At this stage many children rely on verbal counting to solve simple arithmetic problems or a combination of the above strategies. Fingers may be used to represent the objects until children move on to verbal counting where they may be used primarily to help the child keep track of counting. The fingers may be used to represent the numbers being counted as the child raises upright the appropriate number of fingers on either hand and then moves them in succession as they are counted.

Figure 3.1

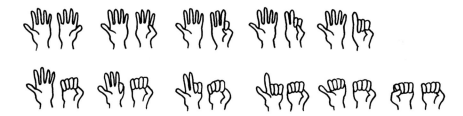

Verbal counting is common in five- to six-year-olds but the shift from the use of concrete representation is gradual and depends on the child's ability to keep track mentally of numbers already counted, as seen above. As noted in chapter 2, there are three basic types of verbal counting:

- counting all of both numbers from one, but not the objects; using the example of 4 + 3: 1, 2, 3, 4 . . . 1, 2, 3 . . . 1, 2, 3, 4, 5, 6, 7;
- counting on from the first number, regardless of its size, which most five- to six-year-olds do;
- counting on from the larger number, which requires understanding that starting with the cardinal value of the larger number is a short-cut although explicit knowledge of commutativity may not be assumed (this is called the MIN strategy).

Five- and six-year olds, similarly, use counting to solve simple subtraction, often using fingers to keep track. When counting up, for example, 7 – 3 can be solved by saying . . . 4, 5, 6, 7 whilst counting fingers, or when counting down by saying . . . 6, 5, 4. These two strategies work well for differences of less than 11; but, for instance, in 21 – 5, children find difficulty in counting backwards and keeping track. Our own research with six- and seven-year-olds – and, in fact, with older children – suggested that whilst they use a 'mix' of strategies for addition and subtraction, most errors occurred from attempts to count down for numbers within 20. Children are better able to keep track of counting without fingers and manipulatives if they count up. Carpenter and Moser (1982) have suggested that children rarely use the counting down procedure because counting backwards and keeping track of counting is hard.

Later, when concrete representations are no longer needed and beyond verbal counting, children will calculate a sum mentally 'in their heads'. The calculation 4 + 3 may be solved simply by saying '7'. Quite how this is done may vary from child to child. Very young children are known to recognise small quantities instantly and it is likely that they generate vivid mental images which may or may not be counted. Later they operate entirely on the basis of spoken words without 'visualising'. As our research showed, at six and seven years – and with many older primary-aged children – fingers are still used to support calculation. In this case there is a very real danger that learning will remain 'procedural' and the effort to execute the sums in question will hinder any growth in understanding operations. From this brief introduction it can be seen that children's early intuition of number develops very slowly into mental 'schema' based on actions, objects and counting which gradually mature into more formal representations.

The scope for making errors at this stage is wide, but provided children's early facility in calculating with small quantities is not mistaken for readiness to carry out formal, written exercises, it is quite likely that errors will be systematic. Ginsburg (1989) has shown that counting errors tend to be systematic, under- or over-counting by one being most common. More often than not, children lose track of which values have been or have not been counted; for instance, 4 + 3 may be solved by counting on 5, 6, 7, 8 – where the child fails to stop after 3. On the other hand, there may be a 'procedural' error: for example, the child does not fully understand the principle of counting on from the larger number and consistently counts in the cardinal value of that larger number so that 4 + 3 is solved by saying 4, 5, 6 . . .

'Derived fact' strategies using memorised facts as the basis for solving more complex problems develop slowly. 'Doubles' facts tend to be learned first: 3 + 3, 5 + 5 and so on. These are then used as a basis for solving other problems: 5 + 6, 5 + 5 + 1 or even 6 + 6. Finally, children begin to use fact retrieval learned through carrying out counting and derived fact strategies. For example, in Figure 3.2, Danny, aged six years one month, demonstrates fact retrieval: 7 – 6 = 1, 'I just knew it', or 13 – 6 = 7, 'I just thought it'. Already at six years of age Danny is using a mix of strategies which ranges from verbal counting, with and without the support of fingers to keep track, memorised facts and derived facts using rules to transform existing numbers and make an easier sum. This response was typical of a group of six- and seven-year-olds assessed in this manner with six mental addition and six mental subtraction tasks using numbers within 10 and 20. In fact, children increased in accuracy from a mean of 7 out of 12 calculations at age six years, to 10 out of 12 at age seven years, with a gradual shift towards more strategies with age. More use was made of the MIN strategy and recall of facts for addition and counting back, with recall of facts for subtraction at seven years.

Figure 3.2

Danny was asked to say how he worked out a number of simple mental arithmetic problems. Each calculation was written on a separate card and he was asked: 'Can you tell me the answer to this sum?' and 'How did you do it?' 'Can you explain?'

7 – 6 = 1	'I just knew it.'
9 – 7 = 2	'I counted in my head.'
10 – 4 = 6	'I counted back in my head.'
13 – 6 = 7	'I just thought it.' [He may be using 'near double' knowledge of 6 + 6 = 12.)
15 – 11 = 4	'I took the five then put one back.' [He may mean that recomposition to 10 has been applied: 15 – 10 – 5 = 4.]
17 – 9 = 8	It was observed that to solve this problem he used his fingers to count back from 17 to 9.

As these two examples show, some facts are easier to retrieve than others, for example, small numbers. Larger number facts which are utilised less often are likely to be learned more slowly and retrieval is likely to be more error-prone. Helpful rules for addition and subtraction may need to be formally taught as children will not necessarily 'invent' them all for themselves (see Figure 3.3).

Figure 3.3

Check whether your children know these strategies for addition:

1 Zero rule: adding with a zero does not change the other number, for instance, 0 + 3 = 3.
2 Number-after rule: the sum of 3 + 1 (or 1 + 3) is the next number in the count after 3.
3 Skip-next-number rule: the sum of, say, 3 + 2 (or 2 + 3) is the number after the next number in the count: 3 . . . 4 . . . 5.
4 Commutativity: addend order does not affect the sum, so that 3 + 2 = 2 + 3 (moreover, there is equivalence between the quantities on either side of the = sign).
5 Doubles plus (or minus) 1: combinations such as 5 + 6 may be considered as doubles, 5 + 5, plus 1 or 6 + 6 minus 1.
6 Doubles by recomposition: sums such as 5 + 3 can be converted into doubles by taking 1 away from the larger number and giving it to the smaller one so that the sum becomes 4 + 4.
7 Recomposition to 10: for combinations such as 9 + 5 the sum can be converted to 10 + 4 because 9 is 1 less than 10.

There is a similar set of rules for subtraction:

1 Minus zero rule: taking zero away from a number leaves it unchanged, for instance, 3 − 0 = 3.
2 Number-before rule: to subtract 1 from a number, say the number in the count sequence which comes before it, for example, 3 − 1 requires the child to think what number comes before 3 when counting.
3 Same-number rule: a number subtracted from itself leaves nothing, for instance, 3 − 3 = 0.
4 The difference-of-one rule: when next-door neighbours in the number sequence are subtracted the difference is always 1.
5 Complements: any subtraction combination can be worked out by recalling its related, or complementary addition combination, for instance, if 7 + 5 = 12, 12 − 7 = 5.
6 Recomposition to 10: for combinations such as 18 − 9 the difference is 18 − 10, plus 1.

(Adapted from Baroody and Standifer, 1993)

Children may make rather different errors when they reach the stage of using fact retrieval. Four kinds of errors have been uncovered (Ashcraft, 1992; Baroody, 1989):

- wild guesses, which are more common with very young children or children working way above their level of understanding;
- near-misses, where children retrieve a 'fact' one above or below the correct fact, which mirrors the earlier-described counting errors;
- operation confusion, where children select the correct answer to an analogous problem;
- table errors, where children answer with the solution to a related problem, for example, for 9 + 4, selecting 12 from the remembered near-fact of 9 + 3 = 12.

As children become more confident with numbers and calculation facts from one operation, they will use them increasingly to solve another operation; for instance, it is possible that complementary addition facts, such as 6 + 3 = 9, will be retrieved to solve 9 – 6. Or, to take another example, the simple 'delete 10' rule may be used to solve 16 – 3 which becomes 6 – 3 = 3 (put back the 10 = 13). Some useful strategies for dealing with larger numbers, however, such as 57 – 24 = 5 – 2 and then 7 – 4 (33) can lead to later 'bugs' if the rule which is generalised is 'always take the smaller from the larger number'. Furthermore, if place value is not firmly learned it is just as likely that the child will reverse the tens and ones (units), which is not possible in the example provided above.

Understanding of whole–part relationships in numbers, in fact, provides the basis for learning number facts – 0 to 5, 5 to 10, 10 to 20, 20 to 100 and beyond – as well as later work with place value and operations of addition, subtraction, multiplication and division. Early understanding of the base-ten system is derived from counting; thus, an important part of understanding two-digit numbers, first to 20 (at six years) and then beyond (at seven years), is counting and number names. Particularly tricky in our system are the 'teens' numbers which place the unit numbers *before* the 'teen'. Initially, then, the system emerges through counting by ones and, beyond 10, in the tens–one structure. Children recognise that '5' and '6' are repeated in '15' and '16' or in '25' and '26', and so on. At the same time they are learning that there may be more efficient ways of calculating than counting. By learning number facts they are also learning to *transform* numbers through 10 to make easier sums, for example, 9 + 4 = 10 + 3 = 13. Obviously, formal teaching must go well beyond counting in ones. Just as knowledge of whole–part relationships of small numbers within 10 supports developing understanding of bigger numbers, counting by tens when learning the numbers to 100 helps the growth in understanding of place value as well as addition and subtraction problem-solving.

Children's fingers can be counted by tens and combined with oral counting in tens – 10, 20, 30, 40 – as well as tens and ones – 10, 20, 30, 40 and 2 – for 42. Number names can be combined with or substituted for base names – 'two tens' 20, 'three tens' 30, 'four tens' 40, and so on. Number lines and grids also help children to recognise number sequences and patterns as well as relate to oral counting. In order for children to begin to understand that counting by tens and ones is the same as counting in ones, representing, or regrouping, with blocks of ten, bundles of rods or sticks, or with similar representations on an overhead transparency, will help children to relate these quantities to spoken or written numbers. Games such as 'Which ten is missing?' and 'What ten comes next?' can, similarly, be played orally or with large number/base name cards; for example, numbers pegged on a washing line (Figure 3.4).

Figure 3.4

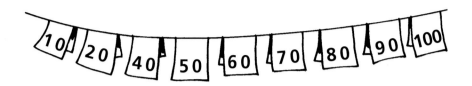

Skip counting on the calculator in ones and tens – 1 + 1 = 2 + 1 = 3 + 1 = 4; 10 + 10 = 20 + 10 = 30 – also helps to reinforce the notion that counting in tens is like counting in ones. Once numbers within 100 – regular and irregular – are well-mastered and understood, numbers beyond 100 are more regular and can also be represented with ten base blocks and units. The question 'How many tens can you make and how many ones (units) over?' can draw attention to the ten-base structure, as does the question 'How many hundreds can you make and how many tens and ones (units) are left over?'

Children's understanding of the ten-base system is important for a number of reasons. Fuson (1990) has demonstrated that it underlies conceptual understanding of both spoken and written, multi-digit numbers. Multi-digit numbers correspondingly influence problem-solving strategies available for solving complex arithmetical problems which require grouping strategies, such as:

$$43 + 38 = \qquad \text{or:} \qquad 79 - 24 =$$
$$43 + 30 + 8 = \qquad\qquad\qquad\quad 79 - 20 - 4 =$$

Without understanding, children will rely on ineffective counting strategies to solve such problems when they are presented orally. Similarly, in the case of the formal, written algorithm: without understanding, children will be mindlessly applying procedures.

Although simple multiplication and division have traditionally been introduced later in the curriculum, in many ways these operations mirror the development of addition and subtraction and, in fact, early multiplication depends heavily on the child's existing knowledge of addition and counting. As noted above, children's knowledge of 'doubles' facts, such as 3 + 3 or 5 + 5, develops early, and when starting to learn multiplication, the repeated addition strategy is an obvious development of this knowledge, 3×3 being set out as 3 + 3 + 3. Similarly children's ability to 'skip count' in twos, threes and fives paves the way for the 'counting-by-n' strategy for multiplication: 3×5 being based on skip counting with the 'multiplicand' the number of times indicated by the 'multiplier' – 3, 6, 9, 12, 15. In other words, by the time that multiplication is introduced, children are already able to retrieve some multiplication facts from long-term memory based on 'doubles' knowledge and skip counting. This will lead to derived facts knowledge: retrieving a related fact from memory, such as $5 \times 5 = 25$, so $6 \times 5 = 25 + 5$. Eventually fact retrieval takes over as children build up multiplication facts over the primary years. As with addition and subtraction, errors in multiplication are likely to be systematic: repeated addition may be carried out once too many times – $3 \times 5 = 5 + 5 + 5$ – or counting-by-n once too often – 5, 10, 15, 20. Retrieval errors commonly result from retrieving the answer to a related problem; for example, 30 (6×5) instead of 35 to solve 7×5.

For division, it is likely that children will rely on their knowledge of addition and multiplication to determine the number of sub-sets of a smaller number (the divisor) within a larger number (the dividend), so that solving $12 \div 2$ might be based on 'doubles' knowledge, such as $6 + 6 = 12$, or skip counting (counting-by-n), 2, 4, 6, 8, 10, 12, or even multiplication knowledge, $6 \times 2 = 12$. Strategies and errors in division appear to follow the same general pattern found in other operations.

An equally important aspect of children's mathematical development involves learning to solve problems which require not only sound counting and arithmetic skills but the ability to use these strategies to solve real-life problems. As noted in the first chapter, development in reading comprehension and working memory as well as the ability to understand and represent the meaning of the problem are all involved. Children's arithmetical problem-solving will be explored in more depth in the next chapter.

What teaching strategies are to be used to ensure that children reach these objectives? Here we can build on the sample lesson in Chapter 2, which introduced maths drama. In this case, it is about people getting on and off a bus, and allows children to imagine their own experience of bus travel. The roles of story-teller (the person who says how many passengers are getting on and off) and actors (the pupils representing the passengers) can be switched to allow various children to contribute their own ideas. As before, the number of passengers is written on the bus, and an arrow drawn in front of the bus indicates direction. When the bus comes to a bus stop, the sign at the stop shows how many people get on or off (Figure 3.5).

Figure 3.5

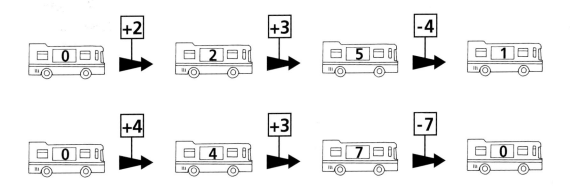

In the context of the buses, the arrow language is used for writing a sum. The drawings therefore imitate addition and subtraction. The bus drawings can then be gradually phased out, leaving numbers and arrows (Figure 3.6). The symbols thus keep their original meanings and therefore the risk of misunderstanding is reduced.

Figure 3.6

In the next example, the symbols are converted back into real-world modelling, to illustrate in a concrete way recomposition to 10: 8 + 2 = 10 + 3 = 13 (Figure 3.7). Another way of illustrating addition is to use a double-decker bus picture and tally marks, as in Figure 3.8: 5 + 5 + 1 = 11. There are more double-decker bus problems in Figure 3.9.

Figure 3.7

Figure 3.8

This is very good preparation for work with number positioning up to 20, using a bead string with beads coloured in groups of five to make a semi-structured number line (see Figure 3.10). The bead string can then be used again later to model the semi-structured number line up to 100.

Conclusion

This chapter began by reviewing successive governments' policies to raise standards in numeracy. In the first chapter we suggested that the relatively poor achievement of English school children in international terms demonstrates

Figure 3.9

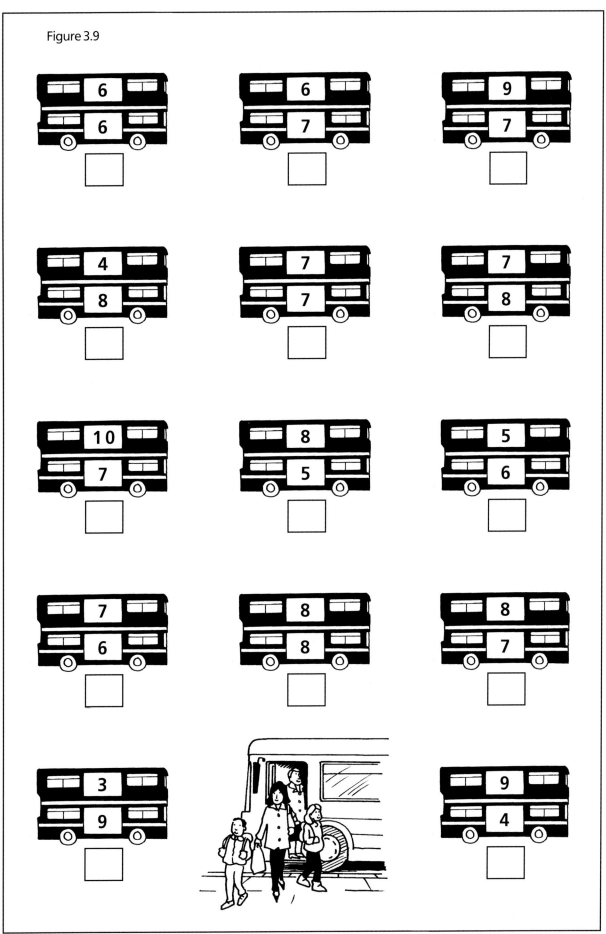

Source: Boswinkel *et al.* (1996)

Figure 3.10

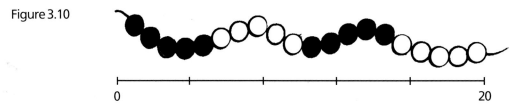

0   20

the need for a better understanding of children's early numerical competence, arithmetic and problem-solving skills as a means to develop more effective ways to teach early mathematics.

To begin with, there does not seem to be any basic disagreement about what should be learned by seven years in the numeracy curriculum here or by our more successful European neighbours; nor is there any disagreement that the strongest influence on arithmetic development is formal education (Geary, 1994; Ginsburg *et al.*, 1981). Furthermore, if we *delay* the introduction of this content it will be necessary to move much more swiftly through this curriculum, as is the case for Slovene children, for instance, who enter school at nearly seven years of age. Our own research has suggested there is considerable evidence of play, flexibility and choice in reception classrooms which has taken too little account of children's existing knowledge and which could be more focused (as is the case in the numeracy strategy).

The challenge is, surely, to develop educational practices which better match the style of young children's learning in the early stages of acquisition. This is more to do with creating a meaningful social context and appropriate materials for action, discussion and the gradual introduction of symbolic number and arithmetic, as this chapter and Chapter 2 have shown. This can be achieved, as our continental neighbours demonstrate, without recourse to written exercises. Furthermore, it is clear from this chapter that, although children are able to recognise pattern and relationships, in order to exploit these mathematically they need to be formally taught rules and procedures as well as have opportunities to practise them. Derived fact strategies may be invented by some children without much explicit instruction but it is unlikely that many pupils will be fortunate or even motivated to *practise* until common number facts are learned thoroughly. Slovenian teachers place much emphasis on repetition and memorising, and this is seen to have an important role to play in the development of automaticity of skill, that is, the ability to perform an operation without thinking about it. This concept of 'automatisation' will be revisited in the next chapter. On the one hand, skill and practice provide a context for learning patterns and regularities; on the other, the degree to which arithmetical facts can be instantly recalled to support problem-solving *reduces* demands otherwise made on working memory. Thus, conceptual and procedural knowledge interact in children's early mathematical development.

In the early stages of development, as Chapter 2 showed, young children – and older ones who are not learning as quickly – develop numerical and arithmetical knowledge from actions on and direct experiences with objects. As competence increases and knowledge of the base-ten system expands, children need similar opportunities to have this system represented in concrete ways. 'Flash math and mental computation' of Payne and Hainker (1993), for example, places various 'tens' rods and 'ones'/units blocks on an overhead transparency for two seconds and children are asked: 'What can you see?' Different combinations can be used and exposure times can be varied. When children have learned to recognise and respond orally with the the relevant number name or base name, mental computation can be introduced. 'What number is two tens more/less?' Two different quantities can be represented on the same transparency and the children challenged to find the difference. As they become more familiar with the base-ten block displays, number names, numerals and base names can be used in a similar way.

To take another example, in the wood-trading game of Baroody and Standifer (1993), children throw two dice, determine the sum and collect the appropriate number of ones/units blocks. These can be traded for base-ten rods or one hundred-blocks; the children are required to keep their own score to 100. Similar games can be made with dominoes and cards. What is important is that practical problems are solved aloud, solution strategies are considered and problem-solving errors discussed and clarified. Informal arithmetic knowledge is the basis for formal, symbolic arithmetic.

Formal concepts need informal investigation. This means that much emphasis is placed on oral and mental methods and there is a corresponding de-emphasis on written exercises. Moreover, oral methods lend themselves to whole-class participation and avoid the danger of wide variation in skill development. In Slovenia not only is written recording avoided before seven years of age but much more emphasis is placed on counting, reasoning and recall through the use of concrete materials, leading to verbal counting strategies and thorough learning of patterns and relationships. The numeracy strategy takes good account of this, but skilful teaching is required. Whilst children may discover doubles facts, such as $6 + 6 = 12$, explicit rule teaching is required to extend the available range of strategies, for instance, to 'near doubles', so that $7 + 6$ is the same as $6 + 6 + 1$. Teaching focuses on patterns and relationships, links these to symbolic arithmetic and then introduces drill to aid recall and transfer. In conclusion, problems are best presented in contexts which are meaningful, solved using as many different strategies as possible and utilising errors to stimulate debate and enhance understanding. Encouraging the search for regularities leads to the formal teaching of rules and the practice of procedures to encourage retention and automaticity. The goals of teaching are always the acquisition of both conceptual and procedural knowledge, which at all times are made explicit to the learners involved.

Figure 3.11

How to assess what children know

Tasks for six- and seven-year-old children: mental calculation

Material:

- Each calculation written on a separate card
- A pile of blocks or unifix cubes

Task: Can you tell me the answer to this sum?
           How did you do it? Can you explain?

Hint: Tell me a bit more?

5 + 3	7 – 6
2 + 7	9 – 7
6 + 9	10 – 4
10 + 8	13 – 6
8 + 13	15 – 11
15 + 6	17 – 9

Criteria for assessing strategies for addition

Scoring	*Description*
0	child has no effective strategy
1	child counts all objects/uses fingers
2	child counts from the first
3	child counts from the larger number (MIN)
4	child recalls a useful fact
5	child transforms number/s

Result: ☐ correct   ☐ incorrect

Remarks:

Criteria for assessing strategies for subtraction

Scoring	Description
0	child has no effective strategy
1	child counts, takes action and counts again
2	child counts back
3	child counts on
4	child recalls a useful fact
5	child tranform number/s

Result: ☐ correct   ☐ incorrect

Remarks:

Figure 3.12

What might a numeracy lesson for seven-year-olds look like?

Jumping backwards and forwards when adding and subtracting

Objectives

- counting on and back in steps of 2, 5 and 10;
- deploying this skill in addition and subtraction;
- practising counting on from the larger number;
- using language: add, total, sum, take away, subtract, difference, altogether, equals.

Context
Dutch children are introduced to the empty number line as a tool for addition and subtraction up to 100. This follows the development line of progressive schematisation of models in problem situations. For example: You are reading a book of 61 pages. You are on page 49. How many pages do you still have to read?

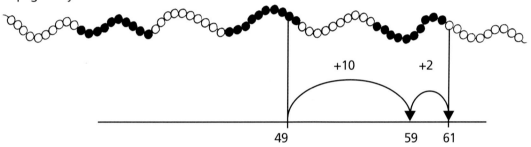

This is rather abstract for six- to seven-year-olds, so they start with a structured number line: first counting up to 20 with beads in the five-structure:

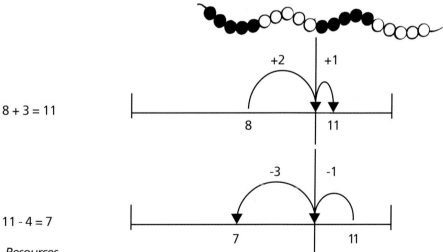

8 + 3 = 11

11 - 4 = 7

Resources

- OHT showing string of beads and empty number line
- individual problem cards showing string of beads and empty number line

Introduction (15 minutes)

Tell the children that today's lesson is about word problems involving adding and subtracting mentally. Start by counting: 0, 5, 10 . . . 50

What's the rule? [Count in fives, increasing and decreasing.]
Now try 1, 3, 6, 9 . . .
What's the rule?
Now try 0, 10, 20 . . . 50
And 50, 48, 46 . . . 0
What's the rule?

Now add tens to the empty number line on the OHT:

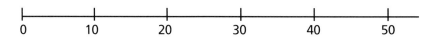

Remind the children that this is used to count on and back or to add and subtract tens by jumping. Practise with: 10 + 10, 20 + 10, 30 + 20.

Introduce examples which do not only have tens, for example: 40 − 18 or 50 − 24.

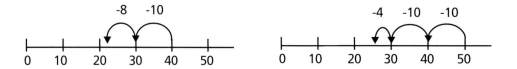

Move on to an example on the chalkboard where neither number is a tens number and ask pupils to draw on the empty number line. Include examples where the smaller number comes first, for example, 11 + 27; 18 + 23.

Talk about putting the big number first: When you add 18 + 23, how do you do it? Is there an easier way?

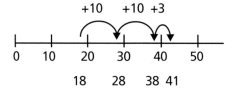

Main activity (20 minutes)
Children work out individual problems using the number line with:

● numbers within 20
● numbers within 50

Challenge
Using an empty number line and bead string, children make their own marks on the line as necessary. Always place this in a problem context. For example, on the school register there are 39 pupils present on Monday, but only 24 are present on Tuesday. How many are away sick?

Plenary (15 minutes)
Work through more examples. Children can describe and compare their strategies.

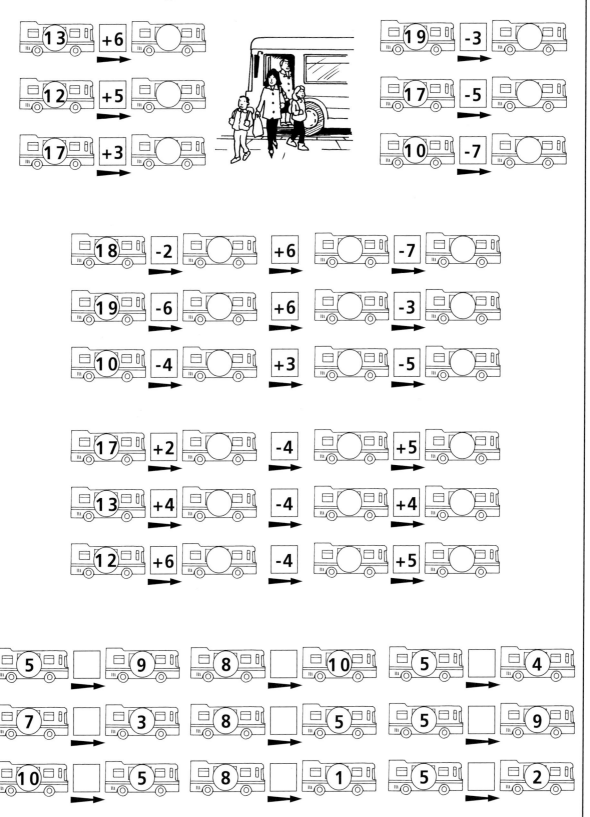

Figure 3.13

Take a bus:

understanding addition, subtraction and difference

Source: Boswinkel *et al.* (1996)

References

Ashcraft, M.H.(1992) 'Cognitive arithmetic: a review of data and theory', *Cognition* 44: 75–106.

Baroody, A.J. (1989) 'Kindergartners' mental addition with single-digit combinations', *Journal for Research in Mathematics Education* 20: 159–72.

Baroody, A.J. and Standifer, D.J. (1993) 'Addition and subtraction in the primary grades', in R.J. Jensen (ed.), *Research Ideas for the Classroom: Early Childhood Mathematics*, London: Macmillan.

Boswinkel, H. *et al.* (1996) *Wis en Reken*, Werkboek 4, Groep 3, Utrecht: Uitgeverij Bekadidact.

Carpenter, T.P and Moser, J.M (1982) 'The development of addition and subtraction problem-solving skills' in T.P. Carpenter, J.M. Moser and T.M. Romberg (Eds) *Addition and Subtraction: A Cognitive Perspective*, Hillsdale NJ: Erlbaum.

Department for Education and Employment (DfEE) (1998) *High Status, High Standards*, Circular No. 4/98, London, DfEE.

DfEE (1997) *Basic Skills for Life*, London: DfEE.

Fuson, K.C. (1990) 'Conceptual structures for multidigit numbers: implications for learning and teaching multidigit addition, subtraction and place value', *Cognition and Instruction* 7: 343–403.

Geary, D. (1994) *Children's Mathematical Development: Research and Practical Applications*, Washington, DC: American Psychological Association.

Ginsburg, H.P. (1989) *Children's Arithmetic: How They Learn it and How You Teach it*, Second edition, Austin TX: PRO-ED.

Ginsburg, H.P., Posner, J.K. and Russell, R.L. (1981) 'The development of knowledge concerning written arithmetic: a cross-cultural study', *International Journal of Psychology* 16: 13–34.

Klein, A.S. (1998) 'Flexibilization of mental arithmetic strategies on a different knowledge base', Utrecht: CDß Press/Freudenthal Institute.

Moser, J.M. and Romberg, T.M. (eds), *Addition and Subtraction: A Cognitive Perspective.* Hillsdale, NJ: Erlbaum.

Nagy, J. (1989) 'Articulation of the pre-school with the primary school in Hungary: an alternative entry model', Hamburg: Unesco Institute of Education.

Payne, J.N. and Hainker, D.M. (1993) 'Early number and numeration', in R.J. Jensen (ed.), *Research Ideas for the Classroom: Early Childhood Mathematics*, London: Macmillan.

Chapter 4

Summing up eight- and nine-year-olds

Introduction

This chapter focuses on the curriculum for eight- to nine-year-olds, in other words, for years 3 and 4. As in previous chapters, we shall include sections on children's learning and development, the processes and content of the numeracy curriculum, as well as teaching and classroom research.

Children's numeracy from early counting of everyday objects and problem-solving in a diversity of everyday situations has already been described in Chapter 2. This led to an examination of the development of more formal arithmetic operations through the use of appropriate manipulative materials. Deliberate connections were made in Chapter 3 between these and the underlying concepts which they are intended to represent.

This chapter will consider the consolidation of arithmetical calculation. More emphasis will be placed on mental representation, problem-solving and introduction of the formal, written algorithm. A characteristic in most areas of mathematics in English classrooms is the widely differing range of attainment which children bring into school and which continues to be a feature of primary mathematics instruction. With a greater emphasis on inclusion (advocated by the Green Paper, 1997) this is unlikely to go away. In fact, this book has sought to advocate sensitive, on-going assessment of individual children's strategies through observation and individual interview as a means of promoting learning for all. In many ways, this mirrors the whole-class interactive approach of the numeracy framework, where teachers ask questions which stimulate explanations, listen carefully to the responses and encourage both the generation of alternative problem-solving strategies and the analysis of errors which are made. Teaching and assessment, thus, require thinking and analysis.

Whether or not, as Reynolds (1996) has averred, the differentiated mathematics curriculum in itself accentuates the 'long trailing edge of under-achievement', our work in conjunction with the University of Ljubljana in Slovenia has revealed that the gap between high- and low-achieving English pupils widens through the junior years. Moreover, in English settings this is particularly evident both for mainstreamed special needs pupils and in areas with high levels of urban social disadvantage. Around a third of our eight- to nine-year-old pupils were unable to attempt the tasks designed for years 3 and 4; instead, they completed tasks designed for years 1 and 2 (for six- and seven-year-olds). These eight- and nine-year-olds were still using the full range of early counting strategies, supported by fingers in many cases, as shown in Figure 4.1.

They could manipulate numbers within 10 and 20 but had no understanding of the base-ten, place-value concepts described in Chapter 3. Furthermore, lower attainers in general lacked strategies for subtraction; they revealed either no effective strategy or frequent efforts to count back, with and without using fingers, which led to losing track of the count, and they showed no awareness of counting on from the smaller number or recall of number facts. In spite of showing effective addition strategies with small numbers, many of these children clearly lacked number sense and appeared to have learned only some arbitrary procedures which were not integrated with or connected to a coherent system of knowledge.

Figure 4.1

Strategies used by six- and seven-year-olds

Addition strategies:

- counting everything (materials or fingers);
- counting from the first number and then counting the second, regardless of the size of the two numbers;
- starting from the larger number and counting on the other number;
- recalling a number fact;
- transforming one or both numbers to make an easier sum.

Subtraction strategies:

- counting the larger set, counting the smaller set and removing it and then counting what is left (materials or fingers);
- counting back down from the larger to the smaller number;
- counting on from the the smaller number;
- recalling a number fact;
- transforming one or both numbers to make an easier sum.

Context

Our own research findings closely reflected those of the 1997 national testing of year 4 pupils (QCA, 1998) which showed that 59 per cent reached the Level 3 standard expected for nine-year-olds. This compares with over 80 per cent of pupils on target at seven years (the end of Key Stage 1) and 62 per cent at eleven years (the end of Key Stage 2). The 1998 figure for pupils at eleven years reaching the expected Level 4 dropped to 59 per cent. This indicated 'if true on a national basis . . . severe underperformance at Year 4' (*ibid.*: 14). Interestingly, this finding can now be seen in the light of OFSTED (1999) reports on the pilot numeracy project, which found that those children who made the greatest progress were in the eight- to nine-year-old age group, and also included a higher than average proportion of those entitled to free school meals.

The performance of nine-year-olds has received very considerable critical attention due to the publication of the Third International Mathematics and Science Study (TIMSS) report (Harris *et al.*, 1997). This placed Slovene pupils significantly above the international norm and English pupils significantly below it, although, interestingly, the Second International Assessment of Educational Progress (IAEP) report (Foxman, 1992) had shown the performance of both English and Slovene pupils to be 'middling'. TIMSS results have already highlighted the important role in high achievement played by whole-class teaching and individualisation in mathematics teaching, as well as the regular use of homework which is typical of central Europe, for instance, in Hungary and Slovenia. Moreover, our own work has reported on the greater emphasis which is placed on mental calculation in continental schools, with particular stress being placed on oral calculation to establish automatisation of number facts. Detailed gradation of successive learning steps is provided in common textbooks and importance is attached to the number of practice exercises at each step (a point highlighted in the last chapter) and to greater continuity in teaching each topic.

By contrast, the English mathematics curriculum has been subjected to continual change for the last ten years. It is broad in scope, including data representation, analysis and geometry. It may be that this broad coverage is achieved at the cost of thoroughly learned and fluent calculation strategies and a developed number sense. Whether or not this is the case, our good achievement in science and relatively better achievement in geometry, for instance, call into question simplistic explanations related to curriculum coverage.

The next section takes a closer look at children's developing calculation strategies.

How do eight- and nine-year-olds develop arithmetic and problem-solving skills?

The arithmetic skills described in the previous chapter provide a foundation for the development of more complex arithmetic and problem-solving skills, just as at a previous stage counting and number underlies developing arithmetic. The relationship between the development of calculation strategies and problem-solving is interactive and varies according to the intricacy of the problem and the size of the quantities involved. Even when children have memorised basic facts and can transform numbers to make an easier sum (see the fourth and fifth points in Figure 4.1), the larger the numbers in the problem, the slower and more error-prone become children's solution strategies. As this is associated with memory retrieval it has been described as the 'problem-size' effect (Ashcraft, 1992). Furthermore, as children learn to solve two- and three-digit number problems, not only efficient calculation strategies but also understanding of place value is essential, as described in Chapter 3.

Although they will be expected to add or subtract any pair of two-digit numbers using knowledge of number facts and place value, at eight and nine years children will be beginning to use the formal, written algorithm to 'record, explain and support partial mental methods' for three-digit number calculation or to check mental methods. This requires understanding of 'carrying' or 'borrowing'. In fact, this skill emerges between six and eight years when children's strategies include counting and regrouping, or decomposition, as well as carrying and borrowing. This usually involves manipulating numbers mentally, that is, remembering the number to be carried whilst writing in the ones/units column. Lack of understanding of place value contributes to the errors made. Sometimes the borrowed number is placed in the line and sometimes a number will be carried unnecessarily when the sum of the units is less than 10.

The regrouping strategy

To solve 35 + 22:
Step 1:   35 = 30 + 5
Step 2:   22 = 20 + 2
Step 3:   30 + 20 = 50
Step 4:   5 + 2 = 7
Step 5:   50 + 7 = 57

The vertical or columnar retrieval

To solve 48 + 27:
Step 1:   8 + 7 = 15 (units)
Step 2:   note carry
Step 3:   4 + 2 = 6 (tens)
Step 4:   6 + 1 (from carry) = 7
Step 5:   combine 7 from tens column with 5 from ones
            (units) column to produce 75

The regrouping strategy

To solve 52 − 29:
Step 1:   29 + 1 = 30
Step 2:   52 − 30 = 22
Step 3:   22 + 1 (from recomposition of 10 in step 1 to produce 23)

The vertical or columnar retrieval

To solve 73 − 54:
Step 1:   13 − 4 = 9 (noting the borrowed 10)

Step 2: reduce (decrement) the tens column
Step 3: $6 - 5 = 1$
Step 4: combine 1 from tens column with 9 from ones (units)
column to produce 19

As is the case for addition, subtraction errors often result from misapplying a rule or procedure, for instance, in $52 - 23 = 31$ the result shows the inappropriate taking of the smaller number from the larger number in the units column. Systematic errors or 'bugs' (VanLehn, 1990) include ignoring the zero in, for instance, $70 - 34 = 44$, and correctly borrowing but failing to reduce the tens column, to take account of this in $70 - 34 = 46$. It is likely that such errors result from a lack of understanding of place value. Early introduction of the written algorithm is likely to lead to reliance on procedural knowledge. Slovenian children learn mental methods thoroughly before any written recording takes place. Ideally, children will add or subtract two-digit numbers mentally, using the vertical method as a check where necessary. Similarly, with two-digit multiplication children will be expected to use regrouping or partition; for instance, 25×4 can be solved by $(20 \times 4) + (5 \times 4)$, executed mentally or supported by written recording.

Whilst children's arithmetic development has been separated from problem-solving skills in the previous section for the purpose of analysis, computation development and problem-solving abilities are closely related. Arithmetic word problems, in fact, represent a fundamental link between developing calculation skills and their application in real-world contexts. In order to investigate the development of children's problem-solving, as well as their errors and difficulties, it is important to examine the growth of their arithmetic skills.

Most word problems have been classified into four main categories, as described in the first two chapters of this book: change, combine, compare and equalise. Furthermore, most of the research conducted has focused on addition and subtraction, although, as can be seen from the corresponding development of the four operations, it is likely that similar general categories apply to multiplication and division. This research provides a clearer view of the way in which children acquire specific mathematical concepts and procedures. Figure 4.2 summarises a taxonomy of problem types and strategies used by children and identifies the major levels of development in addition and subtraction concepts and skills (Geary, 1994: 99), though the numbers used in the problems are very small.

'Change' problems involve actions which children can model with real objects and which create change. The 'combine' and 'compare' problems involve a static relationship which does not require action. 'Equalise' problems are conceptually similar to 'change' problems although the action involved creates a change in the quantity of one of the sets which is constrained by the requirement that both sets must be equal once the action is complete.

Figure 4.2

Classification of arithmetic word problems

Change
  1 Amy had two sweets. Mary gave her three more sweets. How many sweets does Amy have now?
  2 Amy had five sweets. Then she gave three sweets to Mary. How many sweets does Amy have now?
  3 Amy had two sweets. Mary gave her some more sweets. Now Amy has five sweets. How many sweets did Mary give her?
  4 Mary had some sweets. Then she gave two sweets to Amy. Now Mary has three sweets. How many sweets did Mary have in the beginning?

Combine
  1 Amy has two sweets. Mary has three sweets. How many sweets do they have altogether?
  2 Amy has five sweets. Three are chocolate stars and the rest are chocolate hearts. How many chocolate hearts does Amy have?

Compare
  1 Mary has three sweets. Amy has two sweets. How many fewer sweets does Amy have than Mary?
  2 Mary has five sweets. Amy has two sweets. How many more sweets does Mary have than Amy?
  3 Amy has two sweets. Mary has one more sweet than Amy. How many sweets does Mary have?
  4 Amy has two sweets. She has one sweet less than Mary. How many sweets does Mary have?

Equalise
  1 Mary has five sweets. Amy has two sweets. How many sweets does Amy have to buy to have as many sweets as Mary?
  2 Mary has five sweets. Amy has two sweets. How many sweets does Mary have to eat to have as many sweets as Amy?
  3 Mary has five sweets. If she eats three sweets, then she will have as many sweets as Amy. How many sweets does Amy have?
  4 Amy has two sweets. If she buys one more sweet, then she will have the same number of sweets as Mary. How many sweets does Mary have?
  5 Amy has two sweets. If Mary eats one of her sweets, then she will have the same number of sweets as Amy. How many sweets does Mary have?

Furthermore although 'change' and 'combine' problems are equal in calculation demand, differences in the language in which the problems are presented influence the way children represent and interpret and, hence, how they understand what is required and which solution strategies should be used.

Problems are ordered in Figure 4.2 from easiest to most difficult in each category. Most five- and six-year-olds can solve the first two 'change' problems and the first 'combine' problem. The harder problems in these categories, however, as well as the 'compare' problems are still quite hard for six-year-olds. In fact, children are likely to be seven or eight years of age before performance on 'compare' problems significantly increases. 'Equalise' problems cause more difficulty and may not be solved with ease by most children until ten or eleven.

From this brief review it can be seen that children's problem-solving skills develop slowly over the primary years whilst arithmetic and calculation strategies are likewise maturing and becoming more efficient. Children's problem-solving is an area of continuing research interest, and the problems described here are all one-step, routine addition and subtraction problems. This leaves unexamined the problems which require multiplication and division and, perhaps more significantly, non-routine problems which may have alternative but equally valid solutions (see Figure 4.3 for an example).

Figure 4.3

Task: Jaka was counting hens' and pigs' legs. He counted 18. How many hens and pigs does Jaka have?

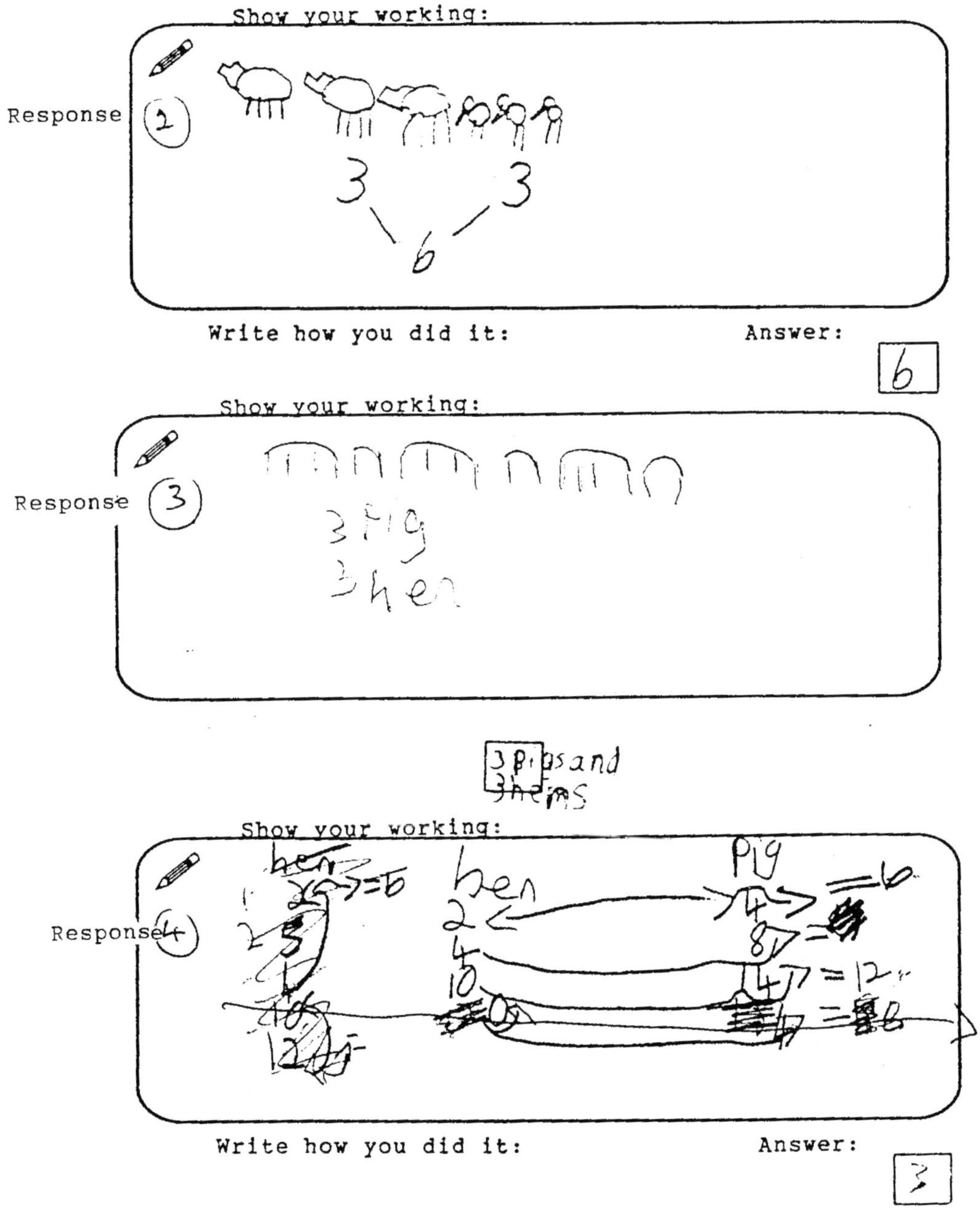

When solving word problems, then, children must match their strategy to a given problem structure by modelling the implied actions (for 'change' or 'equalise' problems) or inferred relationships which determine the quantity of one set by reference to another (in 'compare' and 'combine' problems). Also important is the identification of key words such as 'more' or 'less' which carry mathematical implications for the operation selected. Equally important, however, is children's development of so-called 'schema' or general formulae for selecting and representing or translating the basic meaning of the problem on the basis of 'who?', 'what?' and 'how many?' questions. In other words, problem 'texts' have to be translated into arithmetical equations. As children progress through the primary school it is increasingly likely that problem-solving will be influenced by such factors as reading and comprehension as well as working memory – particularly where emphasis is placed on textbook use. This description of the components of mathematical problem-solving serves to indicate that, whilst it is essential to assess and then extend children's counting and calculation strategies, it is just as critical to improve problem-solving skills, and this may prove more complex. As well as enhancing their basic computational skills, children will need to learn how to identify different problem types, starting with the easiest and gradually extending. Explicit instruction – and practice – on each problem-solving step can combine the teaching and practice of problem-solving steps with problem representation in diagram form on the basis of the 'who, what and why?' schema. Quantity is the most important feature of each problem sentence and the relationship between the quantity/amount that one person has in relation to the other can be shown by relative positions along a horizontal line:

LESS ——————————|———————————————————|—————— MORE
                              person A   person B

Graphic representation in this manner has been found to reduce errors and help develop solution plans.

How does all this add up? A comparison of children's calculation strategies and problem-solving at eight and nine years in the context of England and Slovenia

Turning now to a more detailed examination of the actual performance of English and Slovene pupils on a range of arithmetic and problem-solving tasks, our results were, in fact, more variable than the findings of the TIMSS might have led one to expect.

For eight-year-olds, the trend was for English pupils to score more highly on an untimed, standardised arithmetic test, the British Abilities Scale (BAS). This includes fractions and decimals, which are less familiar to Slovene pupils: they follow a curriculum which places most stress on whole numbers. The Slovene children scored significantly higher on timed arithmetic tasks covering the four operations. English pupils, however, had slightly better scores in problem-solving.

At nine years old, English pupils no longer scored higher on the BAS, and the Slovene pupils continued to score higher for the timed arithmetic test, designed to measure automatisation of number facts. Moreover, Slovene low-achieving pupils scored significantly higher than the high-achieving English group! Again, English pupils scored slightly higher for problem-solving, this time using two parts of the IAEP mathematics scale (see Figures 4.4–4.7).

Figure 4.4

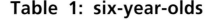

Table 1: six-year-olds

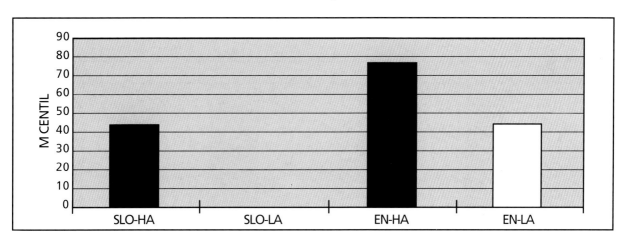

Graph: BAS (Basic Arithmetic Scale)

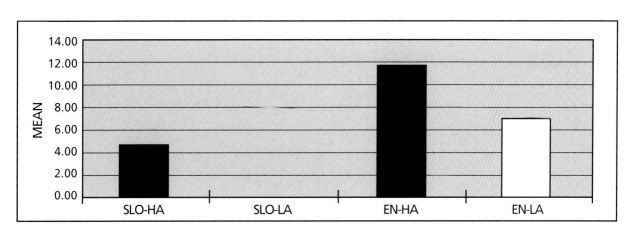

Graph: AAZ (Automatisation of Arithmetic Knowledge)

Figure 4.5

Table 2: seven-year-olds

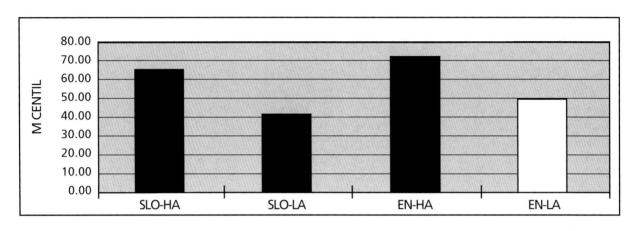

Graph: BAS (Basic Arithmetic Scale)

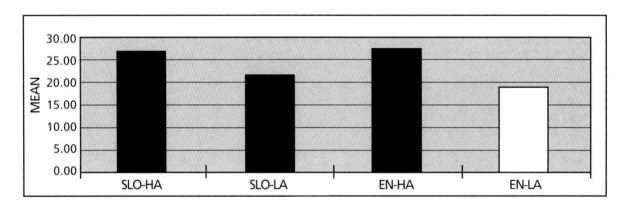

Graph: AAZ (Automatisation of Arithmetic Knowledge)

Key
HA–High achievers
LA–Low achievers

Figure 4.6

Table 3: eight-year-olds

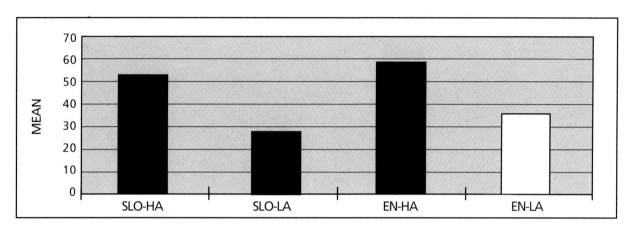

Graph: BAS (Basic Arithmetic Scale)

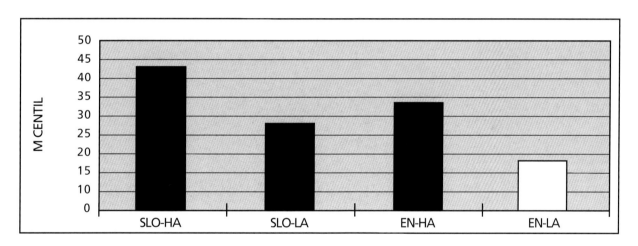

Graph: AAZ (Automatisation of Arithmetic Knowledge)

Figure 4.7

Table 4: nine-year-olds

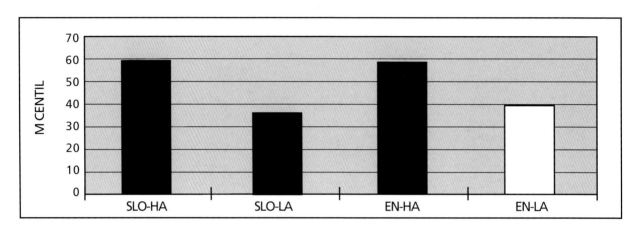

Graph: BAS (Basic Arithmetic Scale)

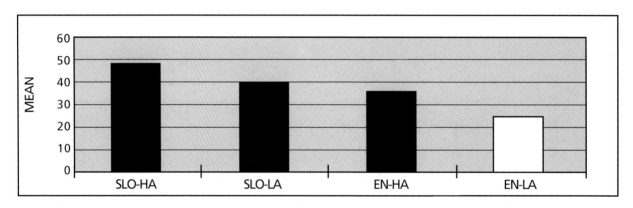

Graph: AAZ (Automatisation of Arithmetic Knowledge)

Bearing in mind the emphasis placed on oral calculation and automatisation of number facts in the Slovene curriculum the results for the timed arithmetic test are not surprising. The slight English advantage on problem-solving tasks may reflect the importance attached to our children's learning mathematical investigations and real-life applications. Taking these findings together, it seems reasonable to conclude that, although sample sizes were quite small, some of the observed differences may indeed reflect different emphases in the curriculum. Specifically, the indications are that more attention is needed in the English context to thorough learning of whole number facts before written calculation is introduced.

Furthermore, in spite of Reynolds's (1996) criticism of the English strategy to offer a differentiated mathematics curriculum and the Slovene preference for whole-class teaching, the gap between high and low attainers in each culture and at each age was significant, reinforcing the view that special measures *do* seem necessary in order to raise the achievement of all low attainers. If, as an earlier section of this chapter has revealed, many of these children are still in the early stages of developing counting and calculation skills, repetition and memorising have an important role to play in providing a context in which to recognise patterns and relationships and hence gain conceptual knowledge. As shown earlier, low-achieving eight- and nine-year-olds in some cases were still mastering number facts and calculation strategies up to 20 and showed a complete lack of understanding of place-value structure and, hence, of numbers 20 to 100 and beyond. In such cases there was a clear need to identify and extend children's existing strategies, with emphasis on oral methods rather than on early introduction of written recording which has the attendant danger that procedural knowledge will be developed without understanding (see Figure 4.8).

Figure 4.8

Errors of nine-year-olds

Greg's solution to $87 - 29$ was: Stephen's solution to $75 - 37$ was:

$(80 - 20) + (9 - 7) = 62$ $(70 - 30) = (7 - 5) = 42$

instead of $87 - 30 (+ 1)$ instead of $75 - 40 (+ 3)$

Both used the decomposition method but over-generalised the rule of taking the small number from the larger one.

Geary (1990) and Geary *et al.* (1987) have shown how children with number difficulties tend to rely on more time-consuming counting strategies, and when a retrieval strategy is used they are less likely to be accurate. As noted earlier, the mix of counting strategies used by low-achieving pupils is more fragile than is the case with their normally-achieving peers and is more likely to be disrupted, with a reversion to inefficient 'count-all' strategies and fingers from the more effective 'count-on' method. Most important to stress is the need for basic facts from 0 to 20 to be mastered so that they are available for retrieval before attention is turned to numbers between 20 and 100 and place value. Again, emphasis on oral methods and concrete representations must *precede* recorded approaches to ensure understanding. If, however, low-achieving pupils have difficulty remembering facts and learning basic mathematical concepts, then the continental approach, to teach one computation strategy thoroughly in the context of developing understanding of place value, may be the best approach to adopt. Beishuizen *et al.* (1997) have shown that two different computational strategies for dealing with two-digit numbers can be distinguished:

- a decompositional strategy, or split method, where both tens and units are split and handled separately, for example, $56 + 22 = (50 + 20) + (6 + 2)$;
- sequential counting, or 'jump' method in which tens are counted up or down from the first, unsplit number, for example, $56 + 22 = 56 + 20 + 2$.

The English early emphasis on written algorithms is likely to have encouraged a decompositional strategy, whilst the Slovene oral tradition favours the development of sequential counting. Moreover, the split method is bound to place greater stress on working memory and increase the tendency to make errors.

Klein, working with Beishuizen, has evaluated the range of materials which have been used since the 1960s to represent the ten-base system. In the 1960s and 1970s, multi-base arithmetic blocks and unifix materials were used. These helped children to gain a strong conceptual decimal structure, but were less effective in helping to promote procedural representation of numbers (Resnick, 1982).

Figure 4.9

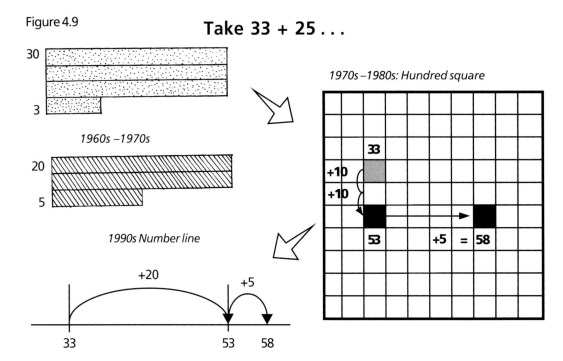

Take 33 + 25 . . .

In the 1980s, the hundred square model was used, which embodied relationships between numbers and allowed visualisation and subtraction operations by the use of arrows or jumps (Beishuizen, 1993). Beishuizen (1989, 1993) found that the arithmetic blocks emphasised the structure of numbers composed of tens and units, and hence decompositional or place-value strategies (the split method, or '1010'):

$30 + 20 = 50$	or	$30 + 20 = 50$
$3 + 5 = 8$		$50 + 3 = 53$
$50 + 8 = 58$		$53 + 5 = 58$

As an alternative to number blocks, however, Beishuizen (1997) has described a linear or horizontal model of number representation up to 100. After a short introduction with a string of coloured beads structured in tens, and with decadal numbers on a corresponding number line, teaching can proceed using an empty format: the empty number line (ENL). Pupils can add their own marks and jumps to support sequential calulation which involves a counting or jump method in which tens are counted up or down from the first unsplit number, with a final adjustment made for the units. This is called the jump method, or 'N10', and was described in more detail in the previous chapter.

Dutch pupils have been observed to progress from counting in units to counting in tens, and later towards even larger jumps, as well as to use the 'split' or decompositional strategy, where both tens and units are split and treated separately. For example, the empty number line can be used to solve the problem: 'Piet has 54 balls. He gets 29 more. How many does he have now?' (see Figure 4.10).

Figure 4.10

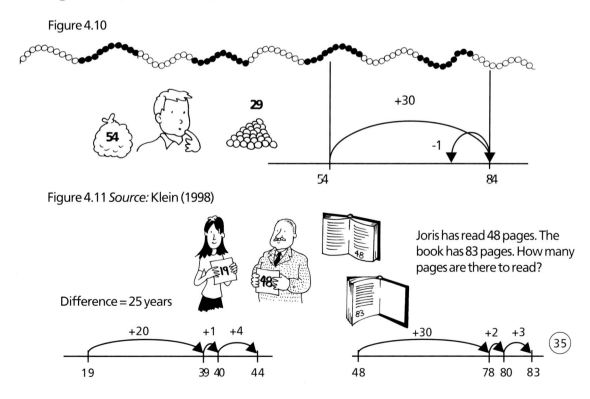

Figure 4.11 *Source:* Klein (1998)

Joris has read 48 pages. The book has 83 pages. How many pages are there to read?

Difference = 25 years

This model allows children to develop their own strategies as well as to devise more sophisticated ones through progressive schematisation. As Klein (1998) has shown, by carrying out problem-centred mental arithmetic in horizontal format, children learn to deal with whole numbers 'as a whole' instead of in parts. In many countries of Europe, however, the 'N10' sequential method is not used in the lower grades. One reason for this is the obvious analogy in the '1010' decomposition procedure in, for instance, 30 + 20, with earlier basic facts, 3 + 2. Dutch research has shown, however, that the hundred square, although providing a better model of the 'N10' method than arithmetic blocks with their 'set' representation of numbers, proves a complicated learning aid for weaker pupils.

Children's own informal methods show quite sophisticated strategies for counting on and back. Gravemeijer (1994) has shown that children prefer the easier adding-on strategy for the subtraction of large numbers – an area of weakness identified from our work for English children. He found that Dutch second-graders (six-year-olds) have more difficulty in solving a problem such as 53 – 45 than a problem situation: 'How many beads are left if you have a jar of 53 and need 45 beads to make a necklace?' To solve this, a counting-down strategy might be used. However, an empty number line allows a simple representation of the problem in a series of 'add-ons'. Gravemeijer also argues that the number line with fixed, pre-given distances for each number is associated with measurements and counting/'reading-off' behaviour. Using a structured bead string as an introductory model for the empty number line will:

- stimulate flexible strategies;
- allow pupils to draw marks for themselves;
- familiarise children with the position of numbers to 100 and the quantities they represent;
- provide tens as a reference point for the jumps to be made.

How to assess what children know

(Based on ideas of assessment by Ian Sugarman, formerly of the Shropshire Mathematics Centre)

Mental calculation

Material: Each calculation is written on a separate card
Task: Can you tell me the answer to this sum?
How do you do it? Can you explain?

25 + 36	64 – 69	7 × 6	56 ÷ 7
35 + 19	75 – 37	23 × 2	96 ÷ 8
62 + 29	87 – 29	6 × 9	64 ÷ 4
129 + 41	112 – 66		

1 Criteria for assessing calculation strategies for addition:

Scoring	*Description*
	a child has no effective strategy (includes written calculation) a child helps him- or herself by counting (includes tallying with fingers) a child carries out the formal written algorithm mentally a child transforms (includes recall of useful facts or partitioning)

Result: correct ☐   partly correct ☐   incorrect ☐

Remarks:

2 Criteria for assessing calculation strategies for subtraction:

Scoring	*Description*
	a child has no effective strategy a child helps him- or herself by counting (includes tallying with fingers) a child mentally carries out the formal written algorithm a child transforms (includes recall of useful facts or partitioning)

Result: correct ☐   partly correct ☐   incorrect ☐

Remarks:

'If a child by no means succeeds in calculating verbally, encourage him to use a pencil and paper to do his calculations.'

3 Criteria for assessing calculation strategies for multiplication:

Scoring	*Description*
	a child has no effective strategy (includes written calculation) a child helps him- or herself by counting (includes tallying with fingers) a child adds the factors a child repeats suitable multiples a child recalls the result

Result: correct ☐   partly correct ☐   incorrect ☐

Remarks:

4 Criteria for assessing calculation strategies for division:

Scoring	*Description*
	a child has no effective strategy (includes written calculations) a child helps him- or herself by counting (counts back using divisor) a child helps him- or herself by multiplication a child recalls the result

Result: correct ☐   partly correct ☐   incorrect ☐

Remarks:

What should children of 8–9 years know about our number system, calculation and problem-solving?

These ideas are taken from the National Numeracy Project

1   Place value, ordering, rounding of whole numbers

- Read and write any number to at least 10,000 (1000 for eight-year-olds); know what each digit represents and partition into thousands, hundreds, tens and units (hundreds, tens and units).
- Count on and back in steps of 1, 10, 100 and 1000 from any whole number (in steps of 1, 10 and 10 from any two and three digit number).
- Add 1, 10, 100 or 1000 to any whole number (say the number that is 1, 10 or 100 more or less than any given two- or three-digit number).
- Use the vocabulary of comparing and ordering numbers (including ordinal numbers); give a number or measure lying between two others and order a set of numbers or measures.
- Use the vocabulary of estimation and approximation; make and justify estimates of numbers up to 500 (to 200); round any two-digit or three-digit number to the nearest 10 or 100.
- Begin to recognise negative numbers in context, for example, on a number line or a temperature scale.
- For nine-year-olds only: multiply or divide a whole number by 10 and begin to multiply by 100.

2   Properties of numbers

- Recognise and extend number sequences formed by starting from any number (to at least 50) and counting in steps of (3, 4, 5) constant size extending beyond zero when counting back.
- Recognise odd and even numbers to 1000 (to 100) and some of their properties.
- Recognise multiples of 2, 3, 4, 5, 10, 100 (two-digit multiples of 2, 5 or 10 and three-digit multiples of 100).

For nine-year-olds only:
- Extend recognition of multiples of 2, 3, 4, 5, 10, 100 beyond the tenth multiple and know and apply tests of divisibility by these numbers.
- Recognise squares of numbers 1 to 10.
- Recognise factors of numbers to 30.

3   Understanding addition and subtraction

- Extend and consolidate understanding of the operation of addition and subtraction, including the relationship between them, and use the associated vocabulary.

● Begin to understand the principles (but not the names) of the commutative and associative laws as they apply to addition and subtraction.

4   Instant recall of addition/subtraction facts

● Know by heart addition and subtraction for all numbers up to 20 and doubles of numbers 1 to 20.
● Begin to know number pairs that total 100.

5   Mental calculation

● Put the larger number first.
● Count on or back in repeated steps of 1, 10, 100 (10, 2 or 5).
● Identify near-doubles, using doubles already known.
● Partition into tens and ones and add the tens first (partition into 5 and a bit when adding 6, 7, 8 or 9 or into tens and units, and recombine).
● Add/subtract 9, 19, 29 … or 11, 21, 31 … by adding/subtracting 10, 20, 30 and adjusting by 1 (add/subtract 9 or 11 by adding/subtracting 10, then adjusting by 1).
● Bridge through 10 or a multiple of 10 and adjust.
● Add several small numbers and look for pairs that total 10 (use patterns of similar calculations).
● Use the relationship between addition and subtraction.
● Use knowledge of number facts and place value to add/subtract a pair of numbers mentally.

6   Pencil and paper procedures: addition and subtraction

● Develop pencil and paper methods to record, explain or support calculations that cannot be done mentally.

7   Understanding multiplication and division

● Extend understanding of the operations of multiplication and division, their effect and their relationship to each other and to addition and subtraction; use the associated vocabulary; understand the principles (but not the names) of the commutative associative and distributive laws as they apply to multiplication and division.
● Develop understanding of a remainder expressed as a whole number; make sensible decisions about rounding up or down after division.

8   Instant recall of multiplication/division facts

● Know by heart multiplication and division facts for the 2, 3, 4, 5, and 10 times tables; doubles of whole numbers to 20, and of multiples of 10, and

the corresponding halves.
● For nine-year-olds only: begin to know multiplication and division facts for the 6, 7, 8 and 9 times table.

9   Mental calculation strategies

● Multiply a number by 10 by moving its digits one place to the left.
● Use related facts and doubling or halving (for example, to multiply by 5, multiply by 10 and then halve; to multiply by 20, multiply by 10 and then double; find 8 times table by doubling the 4 times table; find quarters by halving halves and so on).
● Use closely related known facts (for example, multiply by 9 or 11 by multiplying by 10 and adjusting).
● Partition (for example, $35 \times 4 = (30 \times 4) + (5 \times 4)$).
● Use the relationship between multiplication and division.
● Use knowledge of number facts and place value.

10 Pencil and paper procedures: multiplication and division

● Use pencil and paper methods to record, explain or support mental methods.

11 Checking that results of calculations are reasonable

● Check with the inverse operation.
● Repeat + or × in a different order.
● Check with an equivalent calculation.
● Consider the effect of an operation.
● Approximate by rounding to nearest 10, or 100 for nine-year-olds.
● Use knowledge of sums of odd/even numbers.
● For nine-year-olds only: use tests of divisibility by 2, 3, 4, 5, 10 or 100.

12 Making decisions

● Choose the appropriate number operations to solve number problems and an appropriate way of calculating (mental, pencil and paper, calculator).

13 Reasoning about numbers

● Solve number problems or puzzles, recognise simple patterns and relationships, generalise and make predictions.
● Explain methods and reasoning about numbers (orally or in writing).
● Investigate a general statement about familiar numbers by finding examples that match it.
● Use all four operations to solve word problems involving numbers in real life (money or measures).

Implications for teaching

Children who experience difficulty with calculation are more likely to be successful with instruction which stresses oral counting and calculation, concrete representation of the structure of the arithmetic problem and the place-value system and, if necessary, is partially supported by the horizontal 'jump' method in written form to reduce the memory load. As shown earlier, errors – or 'bugs' – are most likely to reflect lack of place-value understanding and unsuccessful attempts to memorise procedures (see Figure 4.12).

Figure 4.12

What goes wrong?

- Difficulty with symbolism (introducing written exercises too soon).
- 'Bugs' or systematic errors in written calculation which are not picked up
- Unhelpful attitudes or beliefs about what is entailed in learning mathematics ('she expects us to do a lot of sums and to get them right').
- General delay or immaturity (counting, arithmetic and problem-solving which is still at an earlier stage).
- Difficulty remembering facts.
- Difficulty with basic mathematical concepts.

English pupils' slowness observed in timed arithmetic suggests a lack of thoroughly learned facts and efficient strategies. In our study, successful mental calculation solutions were often obtained from the mental application of the formal written algorithm. This again suggests the inappropriate application of procedural knowledge and the lack of flexibility resulting from the early introduction of written methods.

As our small, qualitative international case study shows, differences in national norms may carry implications which extend beyond curricular content and teaching style. As children move through the primary years it is clear that the gap between high and low achievers widens. This will increase if inclusion continues. A developmental assessment and teaching approach is necessary to identify children's current knowledge and strategies in order to consolidate and extend them. Whilst children with learning disabilities may have difficulties in developing concepts, applying procedures and remembering basic number facts (see Figure 4.8), the English emphasis on induction from written exercises is unlikely to be successful with high- or low- achieving pupils. Well-learned counting strategies and basic number combinations applied in a wide range of problem situations which exploit everyday situations may be the most effective means to extend children's knowledge in meaningful ways. Clearly, the Dutch empty-number line method used in conjunction with real-life contexts deals at the same time with both conceptual and procedural aspects of problem-solving.

Figure 4.13

What might a numeracy lesson for eight- to nine-year olds look like?

Objectives

- Extending understanding of the operations of multiplication and division.
- Using addition to discover multiplication facts by doubling a known fact.
- Using language: times, multiply, multiplied by, divided by, multiple, product, count on, count back, sequence.

Introduction (15 minutes)

Take as a starting point a Dutch-type context problem – you could use the dividing out strawberries task from Chapter 1. Present the task on an OHP as words only, without a formal representation (for example, 36 ÷ 3). Ask the pupils to share the strawberries equally among the three children. They should try to solve this in their rough books, for example:

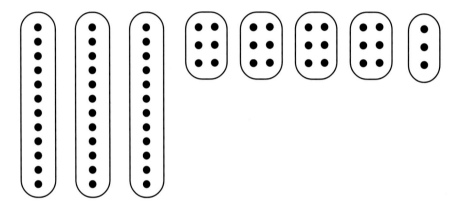

Then ask the children to come up to the OHP and present their strategy or method for creating three equal groups:

- distributing by ones (each time the number of strawberries is reduced by three – distrubutive division);
- distributing by groups of three through asking the question 'How many groups of three can be made?' (ratio division).

Compare methods: Which is the easiest? Which is the quickest? Are there links between the numbers? For instance, $12 \times 3 = 36$; or $10 \times 3 = 30$ and $2 \times 3 = 6$, together make 36. This emphasises the relationship of multiplication to division: by looking at the way you start with a number, then multiply it with another, and end with a third number (the product).

Now practise counting on and back in twos, threes, fours, fives and tens.

Game

- Get the class to count in ones.
- Choose two pupils to sit facing the class: ask one to stand up each time the class comes to a multiple of 2, and the other to stand up each time the class comes to a multiple of 4.
- Repeat with two other pupils and use multiples of 5 and 10.
- Ask the class to monitor the accuracy of responses made.

Main activity
Draw the following diagram on the board:

Task: to colour the sums which equal the number in the centre of the wheel. Ask individual pupils to come to the board and complete the activity. Children can then try individual worksheets:

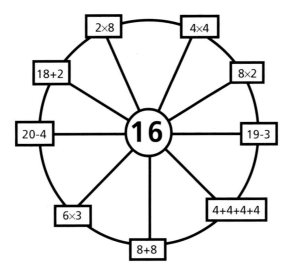

Extension activities

Source: Based on Boswinkel *et al.* (1997)

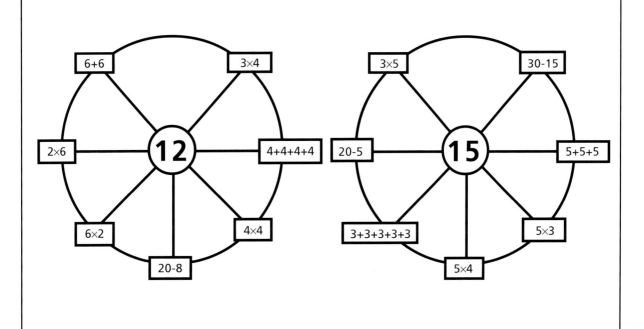

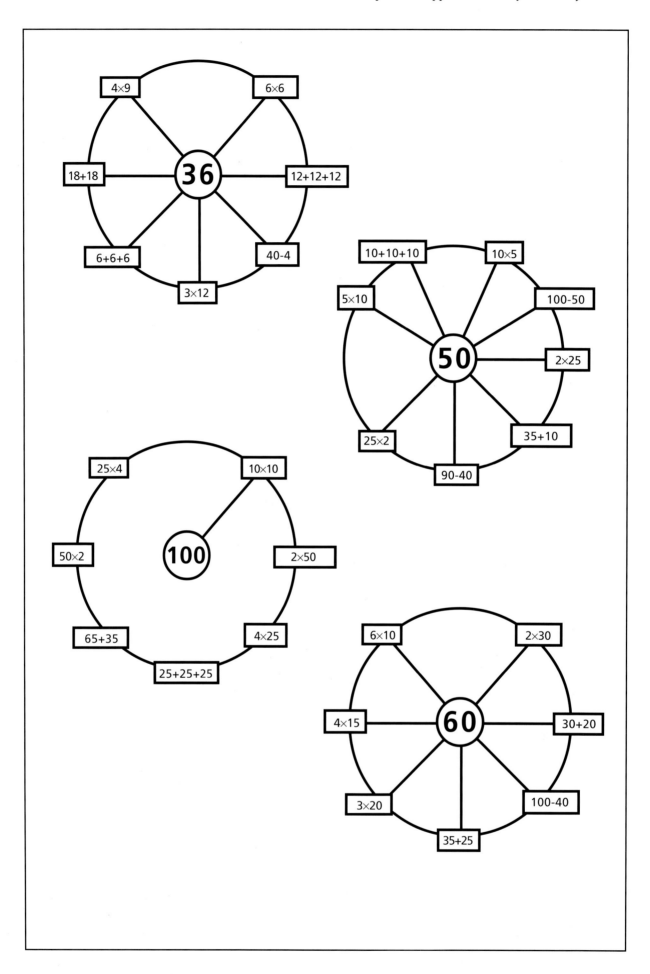

Plenary
Draw the following diagram on the board:

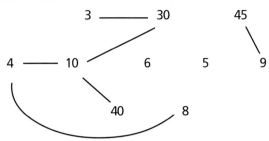

Ask the children to find the links between the numbers and record their answers, for example, $4 \times 10 = 40$; $30 \div 3 = 10$; $45 \div 5 = 9$; double 4 is 8, and so on. Finish with a second context problem, such as the skis problem in Chapter 1 (Figure 1.1).

Commentary
This lesson conceals the way that tables have been learned, which is *not* simply through repeated addition:

5	$1 \times 5 = 5$
5 + 5	$2 \times 5 = 10$
5 + 5 + 5	$3 \times 5 = 15$
5 + 5 + 5 + 5	$4 \times 5 = 20$
5 + 5 + 5 + 5 + 5	$5 \times 5 = 25$

Knowledge is built up through repeated practice. In contrast, Dutch realistic mathematics attempts to include knowledge-building which connects to children's existing knowledge and informal strategies. For example, children learning the six times table might be encouraged to look at a box of eggs – and this could be the stimulus for a problem related to how many eggs there are in *n* boxes:

$1 \times 6 = 6$	you know this already
$2 \times 6 = 12$	you kow this through 6 + 6
$3 \times 6 = 18$	$(2 \times 6) + 6 \ldots$ just adding 6 again
$4 \times 6 = 24$	double 2×6
$5 \times 6 = 30$	half of 10×6
$6 \times 6 = 36$	via $(5 \times 6) + 6 \ldots$ you will soon know this!
$7 \times 6 = 42$	$(6 \times 6) + 6$
$8 \times 6 = 48$	double 4×6
$9 \times 6 = 54$	$(10 \times 6) - 6$
$10 \times 6 = 60$	you know this already

Two models support learning tables: the 'double' number line and the rectangle:

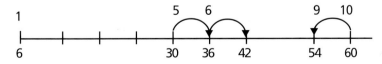

The commutative and distributive properties are clearly illustrated in the rectangle model: $6 \times 7 = 7 \times 6$, and $6 \times 7 = (5 \times 7) + (1 \times 7)$, or $7 \times 6 = (6 \times 6) + (1 \times 6)$. Commutativity is not expressed by the double number line, although ratio is clearly demonstrated, as is the relationship between multiplication and division, which is stressed in the lesson above.

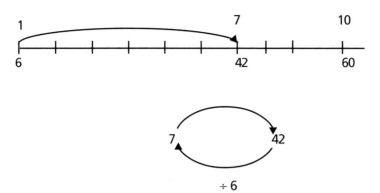

Drill and practice also figure in this approach, which includes short oral sessions, as demonstrated in the lesson. Real-life problems, such as the egg box, which involve packing food items in particular sizes of containers are excellent for developing multiplication skills.

Figure 4.14 **Jumping along the line – addition**
Complete the jumps and write in the numbers

Source: Boswinkel *et al.* (1997)

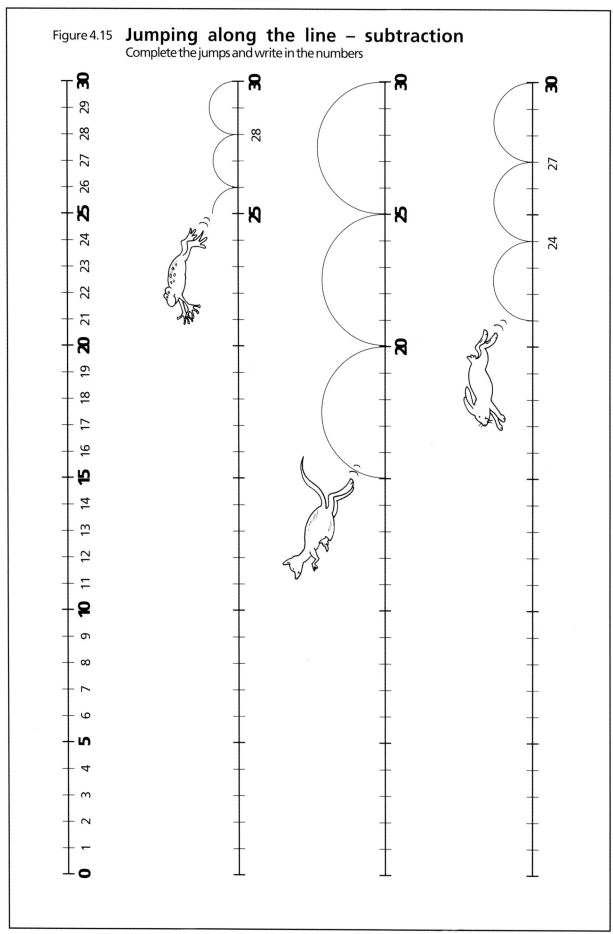

Figure 4.15 **Jumping along the line – subtraction**
Complete the jumps and write in the numbers

Source: Boswinkel *et al.* (1997)

Figure 4.16 **Five ways to make a number**

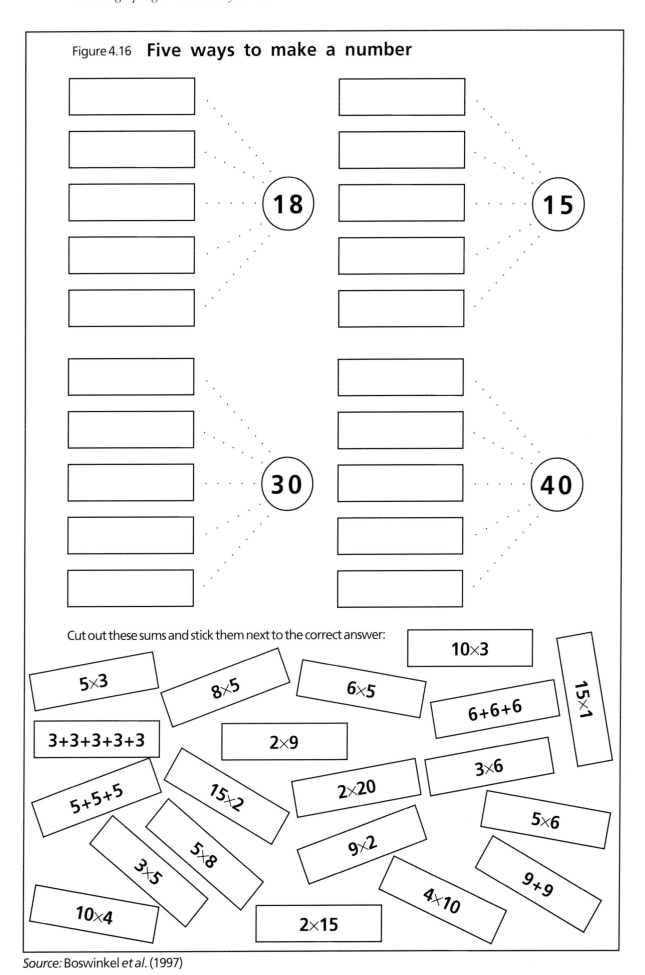

Cut out these sums and stick them next to the correct answer:

10×3

5×3 8×5 6×5

15×1

6+6+6

3+3+3+3+3 2×9

3×6

5+5+5 15×2 2×20

5×6

5×8 9×2

3×5 9+9

4×10

10×4 2×15

Source: Boswinkel *et al.* (1997)

Figure 4.17   **Computations**

If the answer is between 1 and 10, colour the sum green

If the answer is between 11 and 20, colour the sum red

If the answer is between 21 and 30, colour the sum blue

If the answer is between 51 and 60, colour the sum purple

If the answer is between 61 and 70, colour the sum yellow

If the answer is between 71 and 80, colour the sum brown

35+40	70-5	30-29	26+26	40+15	16-8	70-4	48+25
50+15	30+25	12+7	14+14	25+3	7+12	30+28	70-6
25-9	70-65	30-5	36+36	50+24	50-25	12-8	30-16
12+4	20-15	40-12	20+55	65+10	60-35	20-18	30-18
32+32	60-8	24-10	13+13	30-8	30-15	75-20	30+32
80-5	30+35	14-10	28+28	20+38	25-20	34+34	100-25

If the answer is between 1 and 10, colour the sum yellow

If the answer is between 11 and 20, colour the sum orange

If the answer is between 21 and 30, colour the sum red

If the answer is between 31 and 40, colour the sum green

If the answer is between 41 and 50, colour the sum blue

If the answer is between 51 and 60, colour the sum brown

1X5	9X5	4X15	5X3	8X2	6X10	25X2	2X3
2X25	11X3	12X2	5X11	5X12	7X3	4X8	11X4
9X2	6X4	5X8	2X2	4X2	9X4	9X3	6X3
4X3	5X5	4X10	1X10	3X2	10X4	7X4	4X4
10X5	8X4	8X3	12X5	15X4	10X3	8X5	5X10
2X4	4X11	13X4	3X4	7X2	11X5	5X9	3X3

Source: Boswinkel *et al.* (1997)

Figure 4.18 **Calculations**

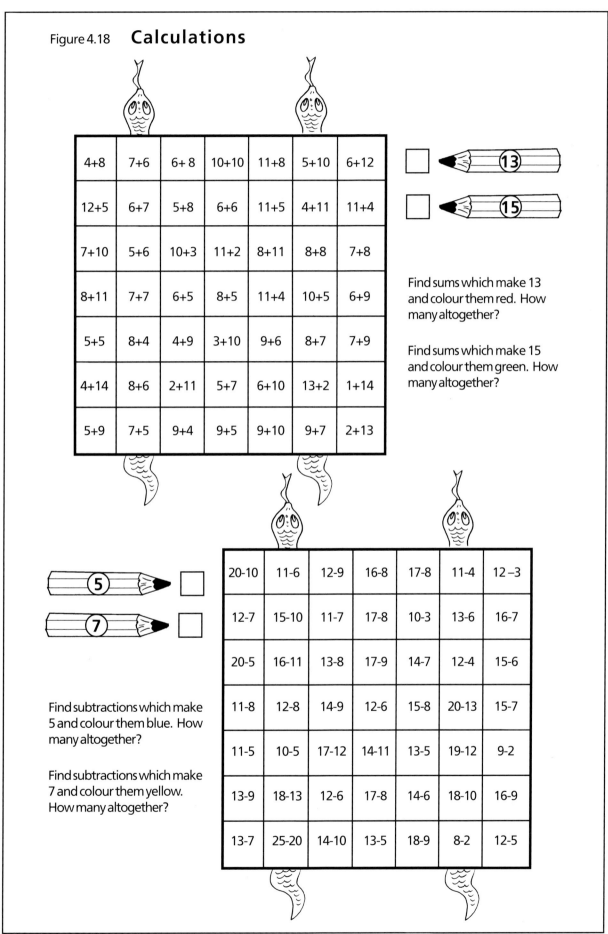

4+8	7+6	6+8	10+10	11+8	5+10	6+12
12+5	6+7	5+8	6+6	11+5	4+11	11+4
7+10	5+6	10+3	11+2	8+11	8+8	7+8
8+11	7+7	6+5	8+5	11+4	10+5	6+9
5+5	8+4	4+9	3+10	9+6	8+7	7+9
4+14	8+6	2+11	5+7	6+10	13+2	1+14
5+9	7+5	9+4	9+5	9+10	9+7	2+13

13

15

Find sums which make 13 and colour them red. How many altogether?

Find sums which make 15 and colour them green. How many altogether?

5

7

Find subtractions which make 5 and colour them blue. How many altogether?

Find subtractions which make 7 and colour them yellow. How many altogether?

20-10	11-6	12-9	16-8	17-8	11-4	12 –3
12-7	15-10	11-7	17-8	10-3	13-6	16-7
20-5	16-11	13-8	17-9	14-7	12-4	15-6
11-8	12-8	14-9	12-6	15-8	20-13	15-7
11-5	10-5	17-12	14-11	13-5	19-12	9-2
13-9	18-13	12-6	17-8	14-6	18-10	16-9
13-7	25-20	14-10	13-5	18-9	8-2	12-5

Figure 4.19

See how many different ways you can answer these questions:

a. How many tennis balls altogether?

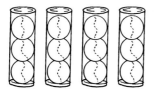

b. How many buns altogether?

c. How many cans of orange altogether?

d. How many candles altogether?

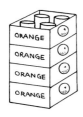

e. How many wheels altogether?

f. How many buns altogether?

g. How many cups altogether?

i. How many cans of orange altogether?

h. How many tennis balls altogether?

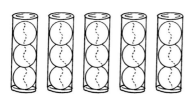

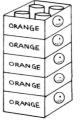

Source: Boswinkel *et al.* (1997)

Figure 4.20

How many glasses in a and b?

How many cups in c and d?

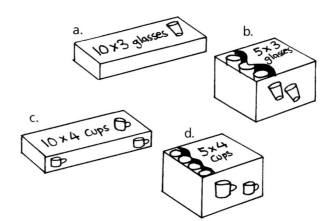

5x4 =	10x3 =	5x3 =
6x4 =	9x3 =	7x3 =
10x4 =	5x4 =	5x3 =
9x4 =	7x4 =	6x3 =
4x3 =	4x6 =	3x3 =
7x2 =	7x3 =	3x7=
3x4 =	10x2 =	10x5 =
8x10 =	2x10 =	9x5 =
6x5 =	5x5 =	6x3 =
9x2 =	8x5 =	4x7 =
8x3 =	8x4 =	7x4 =
4x4 =	3x8 =	5x2 =
2x8 =	7x5 =	2x9 =
10x4 =	6x3 =	9x4 =

Source: Boswinkel *et al.* (1997)

References

Ashcraft, M.H. (1992) 'Cognitive arithmetic: a review of data and theory', *Cognition* 44: 75–106.

Beishuizen, M. (1989) 'Learning addition and subtraction through materialized or schematic representation', paper presented at the European Association for Research on Learning and Instruction conference (EARLI), Madrid.

Beishuizen, M. (1993) 'Mental strategies and materials or models for addition and subtraction up to 100 in Dutch second grades', *Journal for Research in Mathematics Education* 24: 294–323.

Beishuizen, M. and Klein, T. (1996) *Realistic Programme Design*, Leiden, The Netherlands: Leiden University.

Beishuizen, M., van Putten, C.M. and van Mulken, T. (1997) 'Mental arithmetic and strategy use with indirect number problems up to one hundred', *Learning and Instruction* 7 (1): 87–106.

Boswinkel, H. *et al.* (1997) *Wis en Reken*, wisboek b Groep 4, Utrecht: Uitgeverij Bekadidact.

Department for Education and Employment (DfEE) (1997) *Excellence for All Children: Meeting Special Educational Needs*, London: DfEE.

DfEE (1997) *Second International assessment of Educational Progress in Mathematics and Science*, Slough, National Foundation for Educational Research.

Foxman, E. (1992) *Second International Assessment of Educational Progress in Mathematics and Science*, Slough: National Foundation for Educational Research.

Geary, D.C. (1990) 'A componential analysis of an early learning deficit in mathematics', *Journal of Experimental Child Psychology* 49: 363–383.

Geary, D.C. (1994) *Children's Mathematical Development: Research and Practical Applications*, Washington, DC: American Psychological Association.

Geary, D.C., Widaman, K.F., Little, T.D. and van Mulken, T. (1987) 'Cognitive addition: comparison of learning disabled and academically normal elementary school pupils', *Cognitive Development* 2: 249–69.

Gravemeijer, K.P.E. (1991) 'An instruction-theoretical reflection on the use of manipulatives', in L. Streefland (ed.), *Realistic Mathematics Education in Primary School*, Utrecht: Freudenthal Institute, CD-ß Press.

Gravemeijer, K.P.E. (1994) *Developing Realistic Mathematics Education*, CD-ß Press.

Harris, S., Keys, W. and Fernandes, C. (1997) *Third International Mathematics and Science Study: Report on Nine-Year-Olds*, Slough, Bucks.: National Foundation for Educational Research.

Klein, A.S. (1998) *Flexibilisation of Mental Arithmetic Strategies on a Different Knowledge Base*, Utrecht: CD-ß Press.

Nagy, J. (1989) *Articulation of Pre-school with Primary school in Hungary: An Alternative Model*, Hamburg: Unesco Institute of Education.

OFSTED (1999) *The National Numeracy Project, an HMI Evaluation*, London: OFSTED Publications.

Qualifications and Curriculum Authority (QCA) (1998) *Standards at Year 4: English and Mathematics. Report on the Use of Optional Tests with Nine-Year-Olds*, London: QCA.

Reynolds, D. (1996) *Words Apart: A Review of International Surveys of Educational Achievement Involving England*, London: HMSO.

Treffers, A. (1991) 'Didactical background of a mathematics program for primary education', in L. Streetland (Ed.) *Realistic Mathematics Education in Primary Education*, Utrecht: CD-ß Press.

VanLehn, K. (1990) *Mind Bugs: The Origins of Procedural Misconceptions*, Cambridge, Mass.: MIT Press.

Chapter 5

Improving the achievements of ten- and eleven-year-olds with specific difficulties

THE AIM of this book is to demonstrate that knowing more about the way children understand and solve mathematical problems makes us more sensitive to any common errors and misconceptions that are evident in their work and assists us in helping them to generate strategies to resolve them. This requires the teacher to draw children's attention to important aspects of the problem under consideration, to evaluate different solution strategies proposed by the children, and to provide an overview and recapitulation of important teaching/learning points that are being made.

The goal is to teach basic conceptual competence in relation to understanding the base-ten system (conceptual knowledge) and the appropriate use of specific procedures, including equations and algorithms, for solving problems (procedural knowledge). For the last thirty years or so the dominant view has been that approaches to the teaching of mathematics should be founded on mathematical concepts and problem-solving rather than on procedural knowledge, which has been associated with demotivating and inappropriate rote learning. The assumption was made that mechanistic approaches encourage passive learning by the pupil; these were contrasted with active approaches exemplified by the slogan: 'I do and I understand' (Nuffield Mathematics Project, 1967).

The theories of Piaget have also been used to support a belief in children's active learning and the construction of mathematical knowledge in situations where the role of the teacher is to create appropriate materials and a social context within which children 'recreate' mathematical knowledge for themselves. This view holds that mathematical principles are learned in the same way that early counting and other basic numerical activities are developed: through everyday social interactions between care-givers and young children. The danger here is that the planned development of basic cognitive skills may be under-emphasised and the central role of drill and practice in learning rules, deriving facts and fact retrieval may be overlooked.

This does *not* mean simply teaching equations and algorithms. Examination of the close relationship between arithmetical calculation and problem-solving in previous chapters has shown that, where possible, problems can be presented in contexts that are meaningful to the child. Equally, emphasising basic mastery of mathematical procedures, initially with oral–mental methods, leads purposefully to 'automaticity', that is, carrying out a procedure without thinking about it. At this point arithmetic facts will be available for use in problem-solving contexts. The aim then is to solve the problem in as many different ways as possible through class discussion rather than through teaching a formal algorithm. Misconceptions can be discussed, if not anticipated. Thus, errors form the basis for diagnosing difficulties and provide the opportunity to clarify and relearn.

The goal, however, is for all children to develop the same conceptual understanding supported by sound procedural knowledge, and for this to be underpinned by the teacher's clear understanding of the way children acquire these mathematical skills (see Figure 5.1).

Context

As noted in Chapter 1, since the publication of the so-called 'Three Wise Men Report' (Alexander *et al.*, 1992) there has been concern about falling standards as well as debate about classroom practices. This has challenged the autonomy of individual teachers in the selection and preparation of teaching materials which research suggests have encouraged children to learn largely by themselves, often choosing their own strategies and with little whole-class teaching or individual contact. Also noted previously, whilst such methods are intended to stimulate children to learn inductively the patterns and regularities in number and, therefore, conceptual knowledge, less emphasis has been placed on thoroughly learned procedures, recall of facts and, hence, automatisation. In terms of national outcomes on standard assessment tasks (SATs) carried out at the end of the primary years, less than two-thirds of eleven-year-olds have reached the expected Level 4 or above over the last few years, although scores have fluctuated.

Our own small study of English and Slovene ten- and eleven-year-olds showed the same wide range of attainment, with the Slovene pupils maintaining their superior scores for tests of automatisation of number facts at age ten years. None of the differences between the two countries, however, reached the significance level by eleven years of age. Qualitative analysis of selected mental addition and subtraction calculations of two-digit numbers, common to tasks for eight- to eleven-year-olds, showed trends towards greater accuracy in addition for English and Slovene pupils related to age, the Slovene pupils making greater use of efficient derived-fact strategies. For subtraction there were differences between high and low attainers in each country. Slovene high attainers showed the same trend towards increasing accuracy and more efficient strategies with age though low attainers were more variable in accuracy and still showed a mix of strategies. English high attainers showed a trend to greater accuracy using a mix of strategies, whilst low attainers were inaccurate and showed no effective strategies for solving subtraction problems, as was shown for eight- and nine-year-olds and discussed in Chapter 4.

Figure 5.1

Summary of skills

At 10 and 11 years children are:
- consolidating their understanding of place value and knowing what each digit represents;
- comparing and ordering numbers, positive and negative;
- using estimation and approximation of large numbers by rounding to the nearest 10, 100 or 1000.

At the same time, understanding of the properties of numbers increases:
- recognising and extending number sequences, recognising multiples and common multiples, recognising square numbers and their corresponding square roots, and identifying prime factors of a number or prime factors common to two numbers.

In terms of calculation children are:
- consolidating understanding of addition and subtraction, and of multiplication and division, as well as the relationships between them and associated vocabulary.

This includes mental strategies such as:
- using knowledge of number facts and place value to consolidate mental calculation of addition and subtraction, multiplication and division;
- using closely related and already-known facts; for example, $49 \times 6 = (40 \times 6) + (9 \times 6)$, or multiply 29 or 31 by 30 and adjust, or finding the 8×17 table by adding the seven times and ten times table facts.

Pencil and paper procedures will support:
- addition or subtraction of any pair of numbers with up to four digits;
- multiplication of tens and units or hundreds, tens and units by units (short multiplication) or by tens and units (long multiplication);
- division of tens and units or hundreds, tens and units by units (short division) as well as tens and units (long division).

Equally important is checking that the calculation is reasonable by:
- an inverse operation or equivalent calculation;
- calculating in a different order;
- judging the effect of the operation;
- approximating and rounding to the nearest 10 or 100;
- using tests of divisibility, for example, by 2, 3, 4, 5, 10 or 100;
- applying knowledge of sums and products of odd and even numbers.

Finally, making sense of number problems includes:
- using all four operations to solve 'real-life' word problems involving money or measures;
- explaining methods orally and in writing;
- solving numerical problems and puzzles, recognising patterns and relationships as well as generalising and making predictions.

(As in previous chapters, content is selected from the Numeracy Project. For reasons of space and the scope of this book, consideration is given only to whole numbers: fractions, decimals and percentages as well as algebra, measures, and handling and interpreting data are not included.)

In response to low achievement in national and international terms, mathematics educators and policy-makers alike have now recognised the need to introduce a centralised numeracy curriculum and assessment, with specific guidance to provide detailed gradation of successive learning steps and an emphasis on mental methods of calculation and automatisation of basic number facts. Our findings suggest that introducing the strategy to children who have already spent a number of years being taught by traditional means will be a particular challenge to teachers.

Our own work showed the wide gap in skill between high- and low-attaining children as well as marked differences in concentration, application and interest in arithmetic tasks. This was characterised by the use of immature and inefficient counting procedures to solve simple calculation problems and difficulty in memorising and/or retrieval of basic arithmetic facts from long-term memory. Even when facts were retrieved, retrieval was likely to be slow and the error rate high. Such children are likely to need high-quality, teacher-intensive, small-group work in order to make the progress required. But what about the children who appear to have specific difficulty in acquiring numerical and mathematical concepts and skills?

Specific disability

In the literature, it is generally perceived that specific differences between semantic memory and procedural difficulties can be distinguished, leading to the idea that children can have different types of difficulty. Geary (1994) has offered a tentative framework, expanding on earlier work of Strang and Rourke (1985), which includes three distinct sub-types of numerical disability:

- *Sub-type 1: semantic memory* This is characterised by difficulties in arithmetic fact retrieval and problems with memorising arithmetic tables which persist even with extensive drilling and show little year-by-year improvement. Quite commonly this difficulty co-exists with reading difficulty, and is marked by auditory memory problems and poor phonological awareness. Some facts do seem to be retrieved from longer-term memory, but accuracy and solution times are inconsistent. The teacher will probably first be alerted to this problem through lack of progress in reading.
- *Sub-type 2: procedural* This is reflected in difficulties experienced in the use of arithmetic procedures. Whether this simply indicates a developmental delay in the growth of basic number skills or a more general problem of number sequencing or even a delay in acquiring underlying concepts, performance is similar to younger, normally functioning children and tends to improve from year to year if the right help is given. In this case there is no clear association with reading difficulties.
- *Sub-type 3: visuo-spatial* This shows as a disruption in the use of visuo-spatial

skills for the representation and interpretation of arithmetical information, such as rotation and misaligning of numbers. Hence, misinterpretation of numerical information such as place value occurs. This sub-type does not appear to be associated with reading difficulty of the kind described under sub-type 1.

These three sub-types of mathematics disability, however, have so far been described as merely 'best guesses' since understanding such difficulties, and hence introducing remedial strategies, is at an early stage.

For the vast majority of low-achieving children it can be assumed that developmental delays and gaps in learning may be identified by the approach advocated in this book. This approach stresses the need for a fine-grained analysis of existing performance in counting and number, arithmetic and problem-solving (see Figure 5.2) and then teaching directly the necessary conceptual and procedural knowledge.

It is recognised, however, that for a smaller number of children (Badian, 1983, has estimated 6 per cent) more specialised procedures may need to be carried out in order for progress to be made. This will be discussed in the next section.

Figure 5.2

How to analyse children's strategies

Children's problem-solving depends upon:

- a solid grasp of basic number and counting concepts;
- basic arithmetic skills;
- a knowledge of mathematical vocabulary and terms;
- an ability to comprehend or translate linguistic features of the problem into a specific arithmetic operation or operations, that is, to represent the problem and find the best strategy for solving it;
- this process makes demands on working memory.

Analysing children's counting principles
To count effectively the child must master several basic skills to:

- create a one-to-one correspondence between number names and counted items;
- order the number names in the correct sequence (that is, one, two, three . . .);
- understand that the last number named in the count, the cardinal number, holds a special meaning: it represents the total number of counted items.

These principles hold true whatever the objects being counted and irrespective of the order in which they are counted.

Analysing children's methods of addition
Faced with simple problem, for example, $4 + 3 =$:

- do they use concrete materials or fingers and count everything: 1, 2, 3, 4. 1, 2, 3 . 1, 2, 3, 4, 5, 6, 7 – 'the answer is 7'?

Faced with the problem, for example, 2 + 6 = :

- do they count from the first number and then count the second regardless of the size of the two numbers: 1, 2 . . . 3, 4, 5, 6, 7, 8 – 'the answer is 8'?
- or do they count from the larger number and then count on the other number: 6 . 7, 8 . . . 'the answer is 8'?

Faced with the problem 4 + 5 = :

- do they recall a number fact: 4 + 4 = 8, so 4 + 5 = 8 + 1?

Faced with the problem 11 + 5 = :

- do they transform one or both numbers to make an easier sum: 11 + 5 = (10 + 5) + 1 or (10 + 1) + 5 = 16?

Faced with the problem 24 + 36:

- do they split (20 + 30) + (4 + 6) = 60?
- do they 'jump' (24 + 30) + 6 = 60?

Analysing children's methods of subtraction
Faced with the problem 9 – 4 = :

- do they count out the larger number, using manipulatives or fingers, count out the smaller number before removing or taking away the items, and then count what is left?
- do they count back down from the larger number to the smaller number: 9, 8, 7, 6, 5 – 'the answer is 5'?
- or do they count on from the smaller number: 5, 6, 7, 8, 9 – 'the answer is 5'?
- do they recall a number fact: 4 + 4 = 8 and 8 – 4 = 4 so 9 – 4 = 4 + 1?
- do they transform one or both numbers: 10 – 4 = 6 so 9 – 4 = (10 – 4) – 1 = 5?

Faced with the problem 64 – 59 =:

- do they split (60 – 50) + (4 – 9) = 5?
- do they 'jump' (64 – 60) + 1 = 5?

Analysing children's multiplication strategies
Faced with the problem 5 × 3:

- do they use repeated addition: 5 + 5 + 5?
- do they count by 5: 5, 10, 15?
- do they use rules: 3 × 5 = 5 × 3 (or 5 × 0 = 0 and 5 × 1 = 5)?
- do they use derived facts: 5 × 2 = 10, 2 × 5 = 10 and 3 × 5 = 10 + 5?
- do they use fact retrieval: 3 × 5 = 15?

Analysing children's division strategies
Faced with the problem 20 ÷ 4:

- do they use knowledge of multiplication: 5 × 4 = 20?
- do they use knowledge of addition: 4 + 4 + 4 + 4 + 4 = 20?
- do they use derived facts: 4 × 4 = 16 (+ 4) = 20?
- or do they use counting and tally with fingers: counting 1, 2, 3, 4 (with fingers of left hand) and tally 1 with a finger of the right hand; 5, 6, 7, 8 (with fingers of left hand) and tally 2 with fingers of right hand, and so on?

This very rudimentary analysis of children's strategies serves to illustrate that it is difficult to plan effective teaching without knowledge of models of children's arithmetical development, of how these change and of how they relate to the child's observable behaviour in simple arithmetic or problem-solving tasks.

Analysing children's problem-solving
Research is currently underway to identify the skills that underpin children's ability to solve arithmetic word problems and the link between the development of arithmetical skills outlined above and their deployment in real-world contexts. The ability to translate linguistic information into arithmetic terms, to represent it as an operation or operations which can be solved, is complex. It is known, for instance, that the action depicted in the problem is reflected in the strategies used to solve it and, hence, the difficulty of the problem.

Problems such as 'Ben had three sweets, Charlotte gave him two more. How many does he have now?' can be solved by most five- or six-year-olds. Representing the problem with concrete materials answers the question: How many? This is an example of a 'change–join' problem, which has its analogue in a 'change–separate' problem, such as 'Ben had five sweets but gave three to Charlotte. How many does he have now?'

Conceptually different, however, are problems such as 'Ben has two sweets, Charlotte has three sweets. How many sweets do they have altogether?', although they involve the same basic arithmetic. In this so-called 'combine' problem the two sets of sweets remain distinct or 'static' although they are combined in the problem solution as a theoretical, superordinate set. By contrast the change–join problem above involves the action of moving the two sets of sweets together. Such small differences in meaning can influence the way children represent and, hence, solve the problems.

'Compare' problems, such as 'Ben has three sweets, Charlotte has two sweets. How many fewer sweets does Charlotte have than Ben?' are, like combine problems, static because the quantity of the set does not change. In this case the arithmetic operation determines the exact quantity of one set by reference to the other. The compare problem 'Charlotte has two sweets, Ben has two more than Charlotte. How many does he have?' seems more complex. In this case the comparison is less straightforward. In general, children find compare problems harder to solve than change problems. Five- to six-year-olds can solve change problems: compare problems are still hard for six-year-olds. Some, however, like the 'won't get' variety – 'There are three kennels and five dogs. How many dogs won't get a kennel?' – may be solved by pre-schoolers.

Finally, 'equalise' problems, such as 'Ben has two sweets, Charlotte has five. How many sweets does Ben have to buy to have the same?' These problems are like change problems since the operation results in a change in the quantity of one set but the change is constrained by the requirement that both sets become equal after the action has been completed. No such constraint operates in the change problem.

Clearly, in each case children must match their strategy to the problem structure by modelling the actions or relationships that are inferred by the problem. The equalise problem outlined above is solved by children of eight years, but other equalise problems may be found considerably harder. Consider the following: 'Ben has five sweets. If he eats three he will have as many as Charlotte. How many does Charlotte have?' Overall, equalise problems are solved by most ten- and eleven-year-olds.

To solve such problems children must know that some words have arithmetical implications. Put simply, more means add and less means subtract. Yet the compare question 'Ben has two sweets, which is one less than Charlotte. How many does Charlotte have?' requires the child to add, notwithstanding the key word 'less'. Recasting the information provided in order to manipulate it is likely to result in the wrong operation being selected. This still leaves unexamined the non-routine problem, where the appropriate model or solution is neither obvious nor indisputable. For example, 'A farmer is counting the legs of pigs and hens coming into the farmyard. He counts 18 legs. How many pigs and hens does he have?'

The problem-solving examples deal only with small money problems that are suitable for the younger age groups. Children will encounter problems of a variety of types and levels of difficulty during the primary years, such as:

- It is Charlotte's birthday and she holds a party: 4 boy friends and 5 girl friends turn up. How many children are at the party?
- Ben can take three different routes from home to work. How far is the shortest route (in miles)?

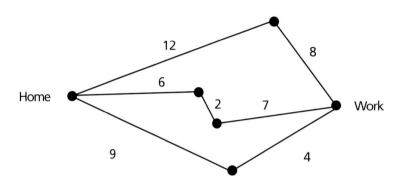

Written methods for complex calculation
Children are taught multi-column problems such as 57 + 94 or 62 – 28 as they move through the primary school. Learning to solve such problems requires not only efficient problem-solving but also understanding of place value and how to carry or 'trade'. In English schools children usually learn to count and calculate first within 10, then within 20 and then within 100. More complex calculations, such as 324,745 + 287,596, are introduced later and, as might be expected, require a formal, written method which involves:

- counting and decomposition or regrouping which depends upon knowledge of place value and associated carrying or borrowing;
- carrying and borrowing, which is difficult for children – and some adults – because it involves:
    - mentally manipulating numbers;
    - making a mental note of the carried number in working memory while writing another number in the appropriate column;
    - understanding place value, that is, knowing, for instance, that the '1' borrowed from the tens column actually represents 10 and not 1.

Such errors are common among US and UK children, but not among children from the Pacific Rim, since Asian-language words for numbers such as 22 (two tens two) make place value obvious.

Improved instruction

It is assumed that developmental delays typical of sub-type 2 can be dealt with by direct instruction in the use of efficient arithmetic procedures and by giving practice in their use, with emphasis on related concepts; for instance, counting principles or useful rules such as 'doubles plus one' or 'counting through ten'.

Developmental difference of sub-type 1 (semantic memory) may, however, be characterised by lack of response to standard interventions. Perhaps more promising here is the provision of alternative means to represent the number system. Geary (1994) has suggested using the Chinese abacus, which represents the place-value system by columns of beads. The bottom four beads represent unit values and are separated from the top bead, which represents five. The abacus can be used to carry out both simple and complex addition by physically moving the position of the beads. With practice it is possible to phase out the use of the beads as mental manipulation of beads in similar calculations takes over (Stigler, 1984). Grauberg (1998) has also advocated the use of non-Hindu Arabic systems such as tallying, counting rods, abacuses and hieroglyphs. It is recommended that recording with tally-sticks or tally-lines should take the form of four vertical tallies with the fifth tally crossing them diagonally or horizontally (Figure 5.3). Five thus becomes the first larger unit of measure. As noted by Grauberg, five seems a good number because:

- it links to five fingers;
- it is half of ten and has a natural anchor point in the decimal system;
- it is regarded as a reasonable size to 'subitise' or recognise instantly.

Figure 5.3

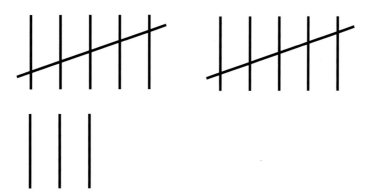

The cuisenaire system has white 1 centimetre rods ('ones'), yellow 5 centimetre rods ('fivers') and orange 10 centimetre rods ('tenners'). Both these systems correspond usefully to coins and notions of exchange (Figure 5.4). The beads of an abacus, in this case the Slavonic abacus, can also be used to present groups of five and ten (Figure 5.5).

Figure 5.4

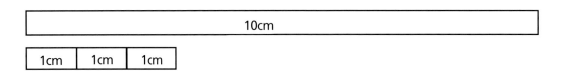

Figure 5.5

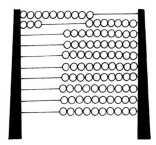

Finally, both Grauberg (1998) and Chinn and Ashcroft (1998) have suggested using the hieroglyphic symbols of ancient Egypt. The advantage of this system is that it represents even very high numbers without a place value and, hence, without the need for zero as the place holder. For instance, Figure 5.6 represents 13 in hieroglyphic number symbols. As noted earlier, the introduction to the empty number line provides a reference point for the ten-base system as well as the possibility for children to map on to their existing knowledge.

Figure 5.6

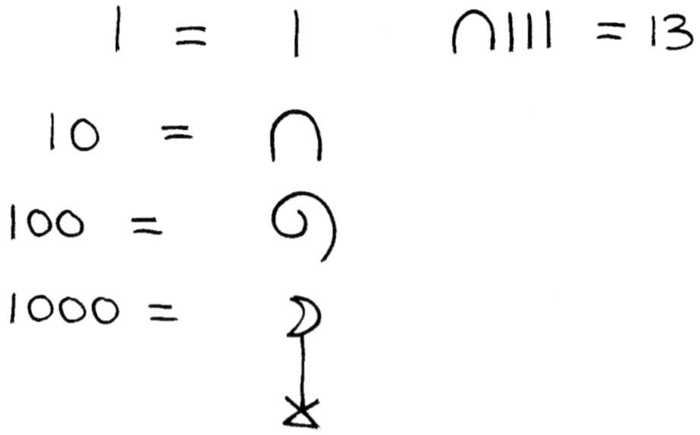

$$ | = | \qquad \cap ||| = 13 $$

$$ 10 = \cap $$

$$ 100 = \text{\Large ℭ} $$

$$ 1000 = $$

Sub-type 3 – visuo-spatial problems – might well also be alleviated by emphasising oral–mental methods aided by alternative representation systems. For formal written algorithms the use of squared paper with visual cues might serve as a further prompt to sequence and direction (see Figure 5.7).

Figure 5.6

h	t	u
	5	4
	2	9
	8	3
100s	10s	1s

Carnine (1997) concludes that low achievement in mathematics has multiple causes and suggests that one may be the mismatch between children's learning characteristics and the design of teaching materials and practices. Design principles better suited to the characteristics of children with learning disabilities have been proposed for five areas:

- teach big ideas;
- teach conspicuous strategies;
- teach efficient use of time;
- give clear, explicit instruction on strategies;
- provide appropriate practice and review.

Since a major goal for all children, including those with learning difficulties, is better problem-solving performance, the application of these principles is thought to be especially appropriate to this area.

The first principle – teach big ideas – is derived from the belief that knowing central ideas within a discipline makes learning subordinate concepts easier and more meaningful. So far this idea has been investigated more thoroughly in science than in mathematics. In the case of problem-solving it is important to introduce formally the different problem types (change, combine, compare and equalise) and to help children to identify them as well as to practise different solution strategies for each.

The second principle – teach conspicuous strategies – enshrines the idea that teaching a series of steps which children can follow to achieve some goal provides an approximation of the steps which experts follow covertly and which can be made overt and explicit for the novice learner. Gradually, as the strategy is mastered, the steps become more covert, as for experts. In relation to problem-solving for different types of word problem, Geary (1994) has advocated that the teacher should:

- state the goal for the problem type;

- provide explicit instruction for each problem-solving step;
- give the child practice on each problem-solving step;
- provide coaching and corrective feedback, where necessary;
- teach how to create diagrams to represent the information making use of who? what? how many? (see Figure 5.8).

Figure 5.8

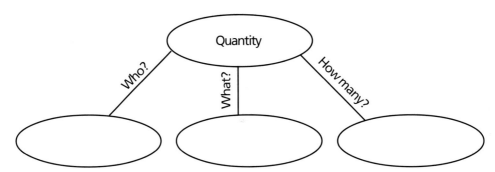

In the 'compare' example: 'Ben has three sweets, Charlotte has two. How many fewer sweets does Charlotte have than Ben?', the information can be represented as in Figure 5.9.

Figure 5.9

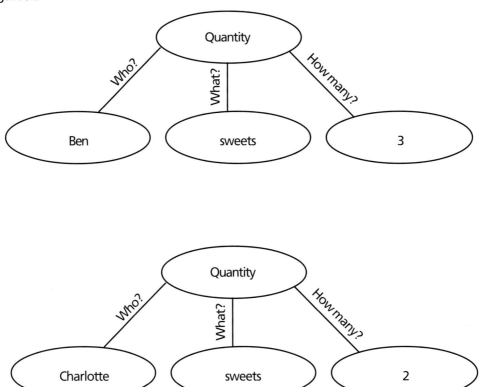

The third principle – use time efficiently – relates to the first principle by emphasising the importance of retaining complexity rather than mindlessly analysing problems into exhaustive steps devoid of meaning and making little attempt to prioritise them in terms of importance.

The fourth principle – clearly communicate strategies in an explicit manner – is a reminder to take account of the child's prior knowledge and to provide a scaffold for the transition to self-directed learning. Verschaffel *et al.* (1997) have outlined a competent problem-solving model underlying the learning environment:

Step 1: Build a mental representation of the problem:
- draw a picture;
- make a list, a scheme or a table;
- distinguish relevant from irrelevant data;
- use 'real-world' knowledge.

Step 2: Decide how to solve the problem:
- make a flow-chart;
- guess and check;
- look for a pattern;
- simplify the numbers.

Step 3: Execute the necessary calculations.

Step 4: Interpret the outcome and formulate an answer.

Step 5: Evaluate the solution.

The fifth principle – provide practice and review to facilitate retention – is a reminder that automaticity is best achieved through adequate practice so that a procedure can be applied or a rule be related to others which contribute to understanding of a new concept. In general, frequent practice is required in the early stages of acquisition; then, as fluency is built up, distributed or spaced practice can be provided.

Timed class or group games with 'link cards' are popular and provide an incentive to learn number facts. Here the focus can be on:

- numbers at different levels (0–10; 0–20; 0–100);
- operations – addition, subtraction, multiplication or division – singly or in combination (addition and subtraction, multiplication and division);
- a number of linked mental calculations designed so that the total for the first calculation, for example, $19 + 47$, provides the stimulus for the next one, for example, $66 - 28$, and so on.

Each child is given a card, and the class or group records the time taken to read out and complete all the calculations. The idea is for each group to try and beat its own previous best time. Alternatively, each child can be given a personal set of cards – the teacher then reads out the calculations and each child then finds and holds up high the answer selected from their set. Again, these may be calculations using numbers at different levels and may cover operations singly or in combination.

Bingo games and dominoes can also be designed to help children practise and learn thoroughly simple number facts. A simple ball game can also work well: a small group of children stand in a semi-circle round the teacher, who then calls out a simple calculation and throws a ball. The selected pupil has both to catch the ball and give the correct answer to the calculation.

Children who have learning difficulties will take a long time to learn to solve problems. Problem types need to be introduced separately and, after initial teaching, mixed with previously introduced problems of a similar type. In summary, a combination of problem-solving scripts and diagrams or drawings may reduce memory load as well as assist in basic computation. The Dutch number line used in conjunction with realistic problems certainly deserves wider dissemination in this country.

Conclusion

Mathematical performance has become an area of intense interest to policy-makers, educationalists, researchers and the general public alike, since it is generally taken for granted that educational achievement and economic success are closely linked. Inevitably styles of learning and teaching have become the subject of debate. Not surprisingly, cultural and educational practices and their relationship to attainment have been closely examined and teaching method is widely regarded as the key. Media scrutiny of such issues has been unprecedented but perhaps more significant has been the bridging of the traditional divide – spatial and conceptual – between researcher and policy-maker, as is evidenced in such Panorama programmes as *Hard Lessons from Abroad* (1996). The potential impact of such research on educational decision-making, judging by the impact of the Channel 4 *Dispatches* programme referred to in Chapter 3, is enormous.

The basic aim of this book, however, is to examine the growth of children's counting, calculation and problem-solving strategies. A subsidiary aim is to examine some of the issues associated with the wide variation in mathematical achievement in order to provide some indication of the way research on children's mathematical development can be used to inform practice and illuminate the learning of special needs pupils in particular.

Whilst broader influences of culture, schooling and family are beyond the scope

Figure 5.10

In summary

Can the child:

- recognise 'how many' in a small group of objects up to five and say which has 'more' and which has 'less' if the group is separated into two sub-groups?
- count 5, 10, 20, 100 objects?
- count in ones, tens, twos, fives, threes, fours?
- read and write numbers to 10, 20, 100, 1000, a million?
- add and subtract numbers mentally to 10, 20, 100 and using written calcuation add and subtract three- and four-digit numbers?
- add several small numbers?
- know by heart pairs of numbers that make 10? pairs of numbers that make 100? pairs of decimals that make 1 (such as 0.6 + 0.4)?
- know pairs of decimals, to two decimal places, that make 1(for example, 0.65 + 0.35)?
- work out simple multiplication with 2, 5, 10, 3, 4? 6, 7, 8, 9, 11? 12? 100? with two-digit numbers using written calculations, for example, 75×8; 394×47?
- work out simple division with 2, 5, 10, 3, 4? 6, 7, 8, 9, 11? 12? 100? with two-digit numbers using written calculations, for example, 75 divided by 8; 394 divided by 47?
- recognise coins and work out what makes 10p, 20p, 50p, £1, £10, £20?
- solve money problems using 2, 3, 5 coins? buying 2, 3, 5 items? involving percentages?
- read time to the hour, half-hour, quarter-hour, nearest five minutes/minute?
- work out time problems using timetables, TV guides?
- measure in centimetres, metres and millimetres; angles to 90 degrees; temperature in Celsius; capacity in litres?
- weigh using scales in kilograms and grams?
- work out areas and perimeters?

Can the teacher:

- identify the level at which the child is showing competence by observing, questioning, examining written responses?
- specify exisiting strategies, errors and misconceptions?
- plan what is the next stage in developing numerical thinking and strategies?
- consider what to provide in terms of real-life problems, models of the structure of number and mathematical thinking strategies, and mathematical language?

of this book, the overview on learning mathematics in school and out is intended to provide both an explanation for and a critique of current practices and reform.

Finally, some indication of the current thinking on mathematics disability is offered and some suggestions to improve performance proposed. Research on children's mathematical development has contributed much to our understanding of learning and teaching as well as individual and developmental differences in numerical and arithmetic skills.

Figure 5.11

What might a numeracy lesson for an eleven-year-old look like?

Objectives

- understand percentage as the number of parts in every 100;
- express fractions or decimals as percentages;
- express percentages as fractions or decimals;
- use key language: fraction, decimal, percentage, half, quarter, three-quarters, equivalent denominator.

Introduction
On the chalkboard write:

$\frac{1}{4}$ $\frac{1}{2}$ 3/5 9/10 18/25 4/50 45/100

Children are asked to:

- order these fractions from smallest to largest;
- say which is the smallest/largest.

Pupils attempt this individually in their rough books and then compare strategies: Can you say how you did this?

The empty number line – or the double number line – can also be used on the chalkboard to express fractions in order of magnitude:

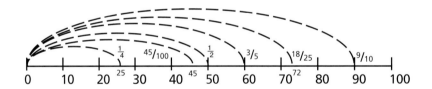

The comparison of fractions can now take place by converting to an equivalent fraction with a denominator of 100:

$\frac{1}{4}$ = 25/100   45/100 already has a denominator of 100 $\frac{1}{2}$ = 50/100
3/5 = 60/100   18/25 = 72/100   4/5 = 80/100   9/10 = 90/100

The fractions may then be converted into percentages (a number out of 100) to compare them. So all these fractions can be expressed as percentages because they already have a denominator of 100:

$\frac{1}{4}$ = 25% 45/100 = 45% $\frac{1}{2}$ = 50% 3/5 = 60% 18/25 = 72% 9/10 = 90%

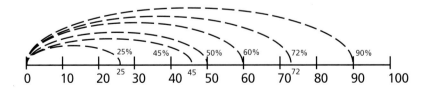

A fraction can also be converted into decimals for comparison:

$\frac{1}{4}$ = 25% or 0.255 (1 divided by 4, or 25 divided by 100)
45/100 = 45% or 0.45   1/2 = 50% or 0.5   3/5 = 60% or 0.6
18/25 = 72% or 0.72   4/55 = 80% or 0.8   9/10 = 90% or 0.9

Main activity from the board (20 minutes)

Complete the table:

Percentage	10	15	30	45	75	100	17
Fraction							
Simplified fraction							
Decimal							

Extension
In pairs, design a bingo game or dominoes using $\frac{1}{4}, \frac{1}{2}, \frac{3}{4}$, 4/5, 7/10.

Plenary (10 minutes)

Class quiz 1 What is:

25% as a fraction?
7/10 as a decimal?
50% as a decimal?
4/5 as a percentage?
70% as a fraction?
0.25 as a fraction?
15% as a decimal?
and so on.

Class quiz 2 Call out fractions and decimals. The children find and display the correct percentage on their number key rings.

Figure 5.12

The number line approach can also be extended to include negative numbers, first from −10 through zero and on to 10, and then from −20 through zero and on to 20.

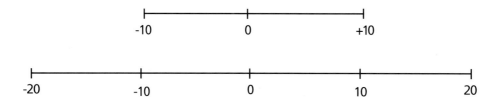

Children can 'jump' forwards and backwards, first in ones, then in twos, fives, and tens. Similarly, decimal numbers which, like whole numbers, use the zero as a place holder, can be represented in this manner, starting with 0.5 intervals and then 0.1 intervals.

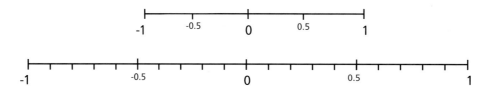

Children can multiply and divide by 10 (also multiples of 10: 100, 1000; and small numbers: 0.2, 0.5) It is likely that children will have encountered both negative numbers and decimals through using their calculators. The number line offers a useful mental model of the underlying concepts and also reduces the risk of errors such as ignoring the decimal point, or misconceptions about the size of decimal numbers relative to the number of decimal places. Helping children to understand decimal place value is likely to increase both their confidence and their ability to interpret decimal calculation solutions sensibly.

By the end of the primary school children will be expected to understand and work with decimals to two places in the context of money and measurement. They need to learn that the numbers after the decimal points do not simple demarcate pounds from pence or centimetres from metres, but that they indicate fractions of the pound or metre unit.

Finally, fractions or percentages can be treated in a similar manner, as can conversions among fractions, decimals and percentages.

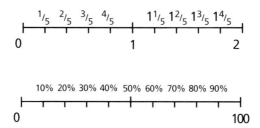

References

Alexander, R., Rose, J. and Woodhead, C. (1992) *Curriculum Organisation and Classroom Practice in Primary Schools: A Discussion Paper*, London: HMSO.

Badian, N.A. (1983) 'Dyscalculia and nonverbal disorders in learning', in H.R. Myklebust (ed.), *Progress in Learning Disabilities*, vol. 5, New York: Stratton, pp. 235–64.

Beishuizen, M. and Anghileri, J. (1999) 'Which mental strategies in the early number curriculum? A comparison of British ideas and Dutch views', *British Educational Research Journal*, 24,5: 519-38

Carnine, D. (1997) 'Instructional design in mathematics for students with learning disabilities', *Journal of Learning Disability* 30 (2): 130–41.

Chinn, S.J. and Ashcroft, J.R. (1998) *Mathematics for Dyslexics: A Teaching Handbook*, Second edition, London: Whurr.

Geary, D. (1994) *Children's Mathematical Development: Research and Practical Applications*, Washington, DC: American Psychological Association.

Grauberg, E. (1998) *Elementary Mathematics and Language Difficulties: A Book for Teachers, Therapists and Parents*, London: Whurr.

Qualifications and Curriculum Authority (QCA) (1998) *Standards at Key Stage 2: English, Mathematics and Science*, London: QCA.

Stigler, J. (1984) 'Mental abacus: the effect of abacus training on Chinese children's mental calculation', *Cognitive Psychology* 16: 145–76.

Strang, J.D. and Rourke, B.P. (1985) 'Arithmetic disability sub-types: the neuropsychological significance of specific arithmetic impairment in childhood', in B.P. Rourke (ed.), *Neuropsychology of Learning Disability: Essentials of Subtype Analysis*, New York: Guilford Press.

Verschaffel, L., de Corte, S., van Vaerenberg, G., Bogaerts, H. and Ratinckx, F. (1997) 'Designing powerful learning environments for knowledge and skill building in mathematics', paper presented at European Association for Research on Learning and Instruction Conference, Athens, August.

Index